Daily

Take ten minutes to transform your life
with Personal Development Retreats
– wherever you are

Volume 1
Retreats 1–20

DES McCABE

NEW ACTIVITY
PUBLICATIONS

Published by New Activity Publications
(a not-for-profit publisher)

ISBN – 978-1-904969-67-9

www.desmccabe.com

For Isabella

Contents

RETREAT 2

RETREAT 3

RETREAT 4

What is a Personal Development Retreat?

When you think of the word *retreat*, what mental images are conjured up? Maybe you think of a quiet place in the mountains where you could rest and recuperate. Or perhaps you picture a monastery or a pilgrimage inviting you to journey inwards to learn more about the meaning of life. Or maybe *retreat* means something more like a health spa at a luxury hotel, a brief but welcome chance to pamper yourself as you take time out from the pressures of modern life.

Retreats have grown dramatically in recent years, with yoga, wellness, meditation, spiritual, adventure, writing, acting and all kinds of experiential retreats becoming part of the mainstream. One reason for their rising popularity might be the level of daily stress and strain that many people are experiencing. More than ever before, we live in an 'always on' culture. Whether your home is in a busy city or a small village in the hills, you probably have access to the internet and the 24-hour global news feed. Maybe it's not so surprising that the need to get away from it all, to reconnect with our sense of self and to refocus on the things that really matter to us, is on the rise.

Many of these retreats also offer a tourist-oriented experience in exotic, far-flung locations. There is often an element of indulgence, combining daily practice with a fabulous holiday. In fact, it's almost as though we have to go somewhere special for the retreat.

But what if you can't head off for a day or a week or a month? And what if you want to make personal development an ongoing priority, rather than a one-off event every so often? This is where the Personal Development Retreats in this book can help. You can experience all the wonderful, inspiring benefits that come with deepening your connection to yourself, to others and to the world you live in, right now, anywhere you choose. No hassle, no planning, no need to find a block of time in a busy life.

How does the Retreat work?

- A Personal Development Retreat lasts for one week and consists of seven short Daily Deflections

- Each Daily Deflection is a short text followed by one or more Personal Development questions to reflect upon

- Your aim is to complete one Daily Deflection each day (typically 10 minutes)

- You capture your thoughts and their key messages in your Journal, or in this book

- You can review your progress at the end of each week and watch your personal development journey unfold

- You can do these Daily Deflections at any time of the day – just try to find somewhere quiet where you can sit without interruption for a few minutes.

Personal Development Retreats are something we can do anytime, anywhere, on our own. They are woven into the day-to-day fabric of our busy lives. We don't need to go somewhere special to get the benefits of contemplation, new perspective and fresh thinking. We can start right now, right here, right where we are.

What are Daily Deflections?

Many of us will be familiar with the concept of *reflection* in personal development, which encourages us to look at, for example, a piece of text, a poem or a quote and think about what it means to us.

Daily Deflections offer us the opportunity to explore further and to see things in a wider context. Whereas a reflection is like looking in a mirror and seeing what we expect to see, a Daily Deflection can help us to move, shift our position and therefore see things – our lives, our future, a situation, possibilities, etc. – from a different place or perspective.

As these Daily Deflections offer us unexpected insights, we have the opportunity to move forward in new ways. We are not just reflecting back to our habitual start point. Daily Deflections can lead us to another perspective in our thinking and outlook.

Each Daily Deflection is about much more than simply reflecting on what we read or think about. It is about reframing and reinterpreting our thoughts, looking in a different direction to allow for a degree of personal realignment. Personal Development Retreats constantly

open up for us new understandings through working with
these deceptively simple Daily Deflections.

My job as a Daily Deflection
is to create
a different thought,
to plant a new seed
and to take you
somewhere else.

My role as a Daily Deflection
is to be there
for you each day,
to offer hope
and encouragement,
and to be a friend to you.

My joy as a Daily Deflection
is when you *see it* ¬–
when you smile
or shed an unexpected tear.
For then, I know we have arrived
together in a new place.

How do Daily Deflections work?

Each Daily Deflection is designed to promote subtle changes in your usual thought process using three key principles:

1. Unexpected Rebounds

The simple process of reading each of the Daily Deflections and thinking about the related questions is similar to throwing a ball at a bumpy or uneven wall. On a smooth surface, the ball will usually *rebound* (reflect) straight back to us. We hardly have to move. Thrown against an uneven wall, however, the ball will be deflected in all sorts of surprising directions. There are bumpy 'Ball Walls' in sports clubs around the world which are used to develop football, hurling and handball skills. The purpose is to help players to sharpen their speed, agility and reactions, and to improve hand-eye coordination. The ball's unpredictable rebound off the uneven surface keeps the player on their toes and open to responding to a range of possible angles.

Like a ball thrown at a bumpy wall, the questions at the end of each Daily Deflection help you work creatively with its content by create unique mental angles, which can give rise to new possibilities within us. Daily Deflections are personal and specific to each individual. The responses I have are going to be completely different to yours. And they are of the moment: if we revisit this same Daily Deflection at another time, we are likely to have a different response.

2. Possible Realignment

The second principle is the opportunity for *realignment*. If we just reflect on something as we usually do, the image comes straight back to us unchanged, as we are in the same mode of thinking. The response from a Daily Deflection, on the other hand, can offer a modified thought, perspective, idea or feeling. Because the rebound brings the thought back at a different angle, we are now invited to realign our position or our thinking in some way. We need to *move*.

Are we going to ignore this thought and just stay where we are? We could do, if that feels right, or we could choose to realign our thinking and say, *Well, hang on, this is interesting... and maybe important. I'm going to talk to my friend / colleague / relative about this idea.*

3. Positive Friction

This potential realignment is produced by the modified thought arriving back to us from an unexpected direction. The backward, forward and sideways shift in our thinking causes *positive friction* because it is a new perspective or reaction that we perhaps hadn't seen or recognised before. Positive friction may feel like a soothing feeling, a gentle realisation or a comforting thought, maybe something like,

Hey, this is actually OK. I'm doing alright with all of this. Or we may instead choose to reject the realignment if it doesn't feel quite right for us at the moment. Positive friction means that whatever we decide, we win, for we can move forward in a better-informed way.

In summary, Daily Deflections are designed to give us an unexpected **rebound** (thought) which can offer an opportunity of **realignment** (movement). The **positive friction** (reaction) involved provides the spark of awareness and energy which allows us to select the direction that feels right for us right now. This is why this simple practice can, at times, feel so powerful: with it, we can realign what we're doing, who we are and where we're going.

One Daily Deflection every day

The core practice is to complete one Daily Deflection every day and to make this a central part of your development. View the Retreat as your interactive personal mentor, helping you to sort out today's challenges, to explore possibilities and to navigate the next stage of life's journey.

There are twenty weekly Retreats in this book. Typically, each Retreat lasts for seven days (one week) and you might focus on one Deflection each day.

Seven out of ten is perfect

You will see that there are ten Daily Deflections available for each weekly Retreat. This is deliberate so that you can, if you wish, choose the seven Daily Deflections that you feel more drawn to, leaving three out.

You can, if you prefer, take two Daily Deflections on some days and so work on all ten in a given Retreat week. The important thing is to spend some time with at least one Daily Deflection each day.

Which Daily Deflections should I leave out?

We are all individuals with our own personal preferences and interests. Some of the topics will immediately chime with you, whereas others may seem less appealing. Try to avoid treating them as a music playlist, where the temptation is to quickly skip through to find a familiar favourite. So often, someone has said to me that the Daily Deflection they expected the least from has given them the greatest insights. This is one reason why some people choose to spend time on all ten Daily Deflections in each Retreat.

When and where should I do the Retreat each day?

Make this practice work for you and your situation. Every one of us deals with various demands from work, family, relationships and all the day-to-day realities of life. Personal Development Retreats are designed to work around you and your circumstances, no matter what they are.

If your schedule allows, it might be worth finding a regular time each day so that you can work the practice seamlessly into your routine. Try to identify spaces in your everyday life where you can create moments of stillness and solitude to engage in meaningful reflection. This could happen very early in the morning, before others are awake, or later in the day when there might be fewer distractions. If you can do the Retreat in your own home, find a favourite chair or room. You might like to be near a window, or maybe you could light a candle to create a little sacred space. Or perhaps a better time for you might be on the way to work, at your desk or during a coffee break.

The wonderful thing about Personal Development Retreats is that they can take place almost anywhere, including the local coffee shop, while waiting for a train, at the library or in a cosy corner of the local bookshop, while visiting a church, sitting in the park or having a quiet drink in a favourite pub. A local park or forest or public garden can offer peaceful places, as can an art gallery or museum, or perhaps sitting by the water's edge. So, use the opportunity when you are out and about to make the most of where you are to deepen your personal development journey. If you do vary your practice location, see if you can observe any differences in the way your thoughts *rebound*.

What happens if I miss a day or two?

Feel free to experiment and play with what works for you. It's important not to feel frustrated if you miss a few days, or disappointed because you haven't been able to stick to your planned routine. This is life after all, and indeed, the feelings that arise may be useful to consider during a Retreat.

The important point is not what you've missed or not done. The secret is to continue, to start again, and to keep going so that you continue to build and grow.

Each deflection is a doorway,
an opportunity to go
to a different room
and see what is there.

Each deflection offers us
an opportunity to journey
with ourselves
in a new way.

Each deflection raises
questions that may need
to be answered
or ignored.

Each deflection offers
a view from a place
we have never been to
or imagined yet.

Each deflection is the voice
of encouragement,
support and kindness
for all that we are facing.

Each deflection challenges us
to be our best self
and to seek
our true purpose.

Each deflection asks us
to look after each other
with kindness and love
always.

Each deflection is
a stepping stone
on our amazing journey
of life.

Each deflection invites us
to move forward
every day
in whatever way we can.

Each deflection is
a message of hope
given to me,
to share with you.

Each deflection invites us
to write down and capture
the wonder that is in this moment,
before it is lost forever.

Use a Journal and capture everything

As you work through these Personal Development Retreats you may notice your thinking becoming gradually more open. You will have some thoughts arising directly from the text or topic, but you will also carry this approach into the rest of your day, stimulating creativity and focus in different aspects of your life and work.

Think about the Personal Development questions. Record your thoughts and ideas. Regularly review all your notes. What are the key messages coming through? What pointers or actions do they suggest for moving forward?

Try to use a Journal right from the outset to capture your ideas and thoughts. Write something in it every time you read one of the Daily Deflections. It doesn't matter if you write just one line, or a random thought or question. It is the writing process that captures and embeds the personal learning to give you the greatest benefits.

As you harvest your thoughts, your Journal will become the ideas hub, source file and launchpad for the next stage of your journey.

17

This book can be your Journal

If you prefer to write directly into this book, there are pages at the end of each Retreat for you to capture a summary of any notes, points and thoughts you want to record.

Retreat Reviews

You will find a Weekly Review page at the end of each Retreat in the book. At this point, take a few moments to reflect on the process over the last seven days, your insights and what you have written in your Journal. All three of these are important for your personal development.

Capture the emerging themes, key notes and progress you've made. These may relate to new learning that you are grateful for, concerns still to be addressed or ideas to be explored further. Write down all of these.

The process of sitting down and doing this Retreat will tell you much about your interaction with yourself. The insights from different Daily Deflections and questions will help you to highlight points that are specifically relevant to you. And your Journal will have captured all that is happening as a visible record of your amazing journey.

Cherish this gathered information and come back to it often.

Daily Deflections are starting points

Remember that this is a book to enjoy. Enjoy these Daily Deflections, which are simply starting points to encourage you to create your perspectives and write the next part of your story.

Allow your thoughts to stay with you after each Daily Deflection is finished. Don't just switch off: take the feelings, perspectives and ideas through into your day. Continue to play with possibilities, and update your Journal during the day with any additional thoughts or insights that may come to you. Keep an open approach to these and welcome them, whatever they are. Try not to prejudge or consciously alter them.

Over time, your Daily Deflections can become a launchpad for your day. Let your Personal Development Retreat be your guide, as it offers the opportunity to connect meaning and purpose with your daily routine and responsibilities. It can bring all the elements of your life together as one enterprise.

Final evaluation and review

This is where we see the bigger picture of what is happening over a longer time period. When you look back at each of your Weekly Reviews, you will be able to see clearly the progress that you have made over recent Personal Development Retreats in the key areas that matter to you.

There may be a couple of clear, obvious themes emerging from the Retreats. Or you may find that several smaller, seemingly unconnected strands have been quietly jostling for position. Is there a way that you can make sense of all this valuable information? You could experiment with blending two or more strands of thought which at first glance seem unrelated. They might be relevant to one another in ways you hadn't noticed before. Take some time and contemplate all the ideas and topics that have formed a part of your Retreat process.

Other ways to use the Retreats

The weekly Retreat format is not set in stone! It's the most common format, but many people adapt the Retreats to suit their way of living and their needs. This is a flexible development process that can evolve around your situation and respond to what's happening with you right now. So, create a practical schedule that works for you – and adjust it as necessary. Some alternative ways to approach the Retreats are set out below:

- **Quick read**

  When we read a famous quotation, we sometimes get a sense of encouragement or hope. Many people will read the Daily Deflection in this way initially, with a similar mindset, to see if it resonates with their own views or aspirations. It's literally only a couple of minutes every day.

- **10-day cycle**

  Another approach is to take one Daily Deflection each day (around 10¬–15 minutes) and work your way through the entire book, completing all of the Daily Deflections without pausing for breath! If you have some extra time right now, this is a great way to work through the issues in an immediate and unself-conscious way.

- **Monthly Retreat**

  Some people decide on different fixed timescales at the outset (30 days, for example) and allocate 15–20 minutes per day to explore some of the themes and perspectives in this book using this more deliberate and focused method.

- **Morning and evening**

  Others have chosen two different Daily Deflections to work with each day (typically one in the morning and another in the evening). You may find the Contents page useful in choosing your Daily Deflections.

- **In our workplaces**

  The Daily Deflections may enable us to build understanding within our group, team, business or community at a much deeper level. By using the Daily Deflections individually at first and then collectively, we can enable individuals to step outside of their typical role in the workplace.

Now it's time to get started on your Personal Development Retreats.

Personal Development Retreat

1

What is personal asset management?

Interest Rates

What is your level of interest
in the job that you do?
Do you give your best in every situation
and to every person?

Do you encourage, motivate
and inspire others?
Are you positive,
enthusiastic and helpful?

Do you always give 100%
to the work that you do?
If we can increase our interest rate,
we'll all enjoy greater returns.

DAILY DEFLECTION – QUESTIONS

1. Where are you investing your time, energy and experience?

2. What are the key relationships that you want to invest more into?

3. How will you measure your returns?

Who are the entrepreneurs of life?

Entrepreneurship

We are the entrepreneurs of life,
not slaves of the past
or prisoners of expectation.

We are the entrepreneurs of life,
looking after all our global neighbours
and caring for our beautiful world.

We are the entrepreneurs of life,
rethinking, creating, shaping and building
a different way, in our own way.

We are the glorious, beautiful,
gentle, kind, visionary
and successful entrepreneurs of life.

DAILY DEFLECTION – QUESTIONS

1. Entrepreneurship relates to all aspects of our lives – not just business creation.

2. Can you think of five areas, ways, situations or relationships where you could be more entrepreneurial?

Can business and spirituality sit together?

Currency Flipping

Some say that
business is about doing
and
spirituality is about being.

These are the two sides
of the coin of life – doing and being.
They sit together
within each of us.

But the two sides face
in opposite directions
so, unfortunately,
cannot be viewed at the same time.

We have to consciously choose
to flip over the coin.
Then we get the full picture for a moment.
We see everything in totality.

But what if we could sit
on the edge of the coin
and touch both sides together
at the same time?

Doing and being.
The edge of the coin.
Business and spirituality
as one.

DAILY DEFLECTION – QUESTIONS

1. In a sentence, write down what spirituality means to you.

2. The language of business is different from the language of spirituality. Make a list of five words for business and five for spirituality, each of which is rarely used in the other area.

3. How might business and spirituality link together to create new perspectives, questions and opportunities for all?

What is your personal interest rate?

Interest Rates

What is your level of interest
in the job that you do?
Do you give your best in every situation
and to every person?

Do you encourage, motivate
and inspire others?
Are you positive,
enthusiastic and helpful?

Do you always give 100%
to the work that you do?
If we can increase our interest rate,
we'll all enjoy greater returns.

DAILY DEFLECTION – QUESTIONS

1. Where are you investing your time, energy and experience?

2. What are the key relationships that you want to invest more into?

3. How will you measure your returns?

What is really going on at recycling centres?

Disrupt the Transaction

Saturday morning at the recycling centre
was well organised.
I found the right skips and dropped in
the old rug and some bits of wood.

Feeling a sense of relief to have
completed the task,
I said to a fellow visitor,
'Great to get rid of it, isn't it?'

He replied, 'I hate this job.'
'But there's a sense of getting it done,
isn't there?' I replied,
as we walked back to our cars.

'It's taken me a year to get round to this
after my mum died...' he said quietly.
'And then I will have to start
on my own house...'

'Look after yourself,' I said,
as we got into our cars.
'You too, mate,' he said.
We both nodded and smiled softly.

DAILY DEFLECTION – QUESTIONS

1. How might you be more empathetic towards others?

2. How can you disrupt everyday transactions and turn them into positive interactions?

Where is the profit in spirituality?

Profits

We are all called as prophets when we are born:
to stand up for what is right, to go against the crowd
and to give a voice to those who have none.

We are all called to use our talents and gifts in all
moments and in all circumstances; gifts of listening,
writing, speaking, fixing, making and organising.

We are all called to learn from our experience as we
journey, for wisdom is the fruit of age. It needs the
nourishment of continuing along the right path.

We are all called for a purpose.
Today has its purpose for us
and we must seek it with all of our being.

We are all called to be with God – not in some
religious way that is detached from the 'real' world,
but in a way that goes to the heart of our very being.

We are all called as prophets – to be truly ourselves.

DAILY DEFLECTION – QUESTIONS

1. What does the word *profit* mean to you?

2. What does the word *prophet* mean to you?

3. Where (if any) are the points of overlap?

How can you become a social influencer?

Social Influencers

In this new era of remote working,
send out your message of kindness
on Facebook, Twitter, LinkedIn,
YouTube, Instagram or TikTok.

You can change lives
with your encouragement, stories,
experience, guidance or expertise.
And you may never know about it.

So, do not worry about likes,
shares or feedback.
Those who need your help
or advice will find you.

The approval of others is irrelevant,
for this is only vanity.
Capture your thoughts, be brave
and put your love out there.

Remember, the biggest 'like' is yourself,
and valuing all that you are.
The biggest 'share' is when you
offer this to everyone.

DAILY DEFLECTION – QUESTIONS

Fifty years ago, Joe Karbo said that each of us knows more about something than half of the people in the world.

1. What is your area of experience?

2. How can you help others?

3. How will you share your expertise?

How do I write a kindness policy?

Policy Review

Life is hard for many people.
We lose those we love.
We suffer personal disappointments and setbacks.
We struggle to pay for the things we need.
We worry about those close to us.

Most of this, people carry to work,
where little is said.

Kindness is the foundation of well-being.
It's a gentle way of being.
It's helping when you can, without being asked.
It's checking quietly if all is okay.
It's time to write our Kindness Policy.

DAILY DEFLECTION – QUESTIONS

1. Draft a Kindness Policy for your workplace, group or family.

2. What is the purpose of the Policy?

3. How will it work?

4. What should it achieve?

What type of leader are you?

Household Management

Lightbulb Managers:
Visionaries with a caring and responsive approach to others.
They shine.
They provide inspiration for others.
They are most visible when things are tough.
They respond immediately.
They are consistent.
They do not discriminate with their support.

Wardrobe Managers:
They possess strong organisational, presentation and personal development skills.
They review their objectives every morning.
They plan their weeks in advance.
They regularly add new skills and review resources.
They clear out the dead wood as required.
They are very aware of first impressions.

Attic Managers:

They are seen as largely inaccessible and irrelevant in today's business.

They hoard, taking rather than giving.

They work in the dark.

They are locked away and are rarely seen.

They are held with some sentimental value until the Big Clear-Out.

They relate best to children and older people.

They cherish only the past.

DAILY DEFLECTION – QUESTIONS

1. What type of Household Manager are you?

2. Can you create another house-related category that reflects different attitudes, behaviours or aspects of management?

Who are you?

Management Buyout

I reinvented my life today.
I created a whole new way of being.
I redefined who I am
and what I am about.
I left behind my old life,
my previous world.

I still know all the same people
but I see them through different glasses now,
clearer and brighter.
Today, I created a whole new way of being.
I'm a different person
in the same skin.

DAILY DEFLECTION – QUESTIONS

1. If you were to reinvent your life today, what would it look like?

2. What is your new way of being?

Retreat 1 – Notes and Key Points

Day 1

_____

_____

_____

Day 2

_____

_____

_____

Day 3

_____

_____

_____

Day 4

_____

_____

_____

Day 5

_____

_____

_____

Day 6

_____

_____

_____

Day 7

_____

_____

_____

Overall thoughts about the week

_____

_____

_____

_____

Points to take with me on the journey

_____

_____

_____

_____

Personal Development Retreat

2

How can I build real wealth?

Wealth Creation

The contract for sharing,
called the *seller and buyer*,
is flawed because it involves
the exchange of money.

This excludes so many
who wish to benefit
from your products,
services or experience.

People may never know
the value of what you can offer,
or simply may not
have the money to buy.

They may live in
other parts of the world
where the cost of your expertise
is beyond their reach.

Give away your stuff for free,
build real relationships
and create a sharing global economy
where all can participate equally.

For your real wealth lies
not in limited financial transactions
but in the spread of your gifts
outwards and onwards, forever.

DAILY DEFLECTION – QUESTIONS

1. What are the three greatest gifts (knowledge, experience or expertise) that you have been blessed with?

2. How can you begin today to share just one of these with others for free?

How can I hit my target?

Hitting Targets

If you throw a stone
to hit a stick in the water,
you can easily miss.
Try again.

If you keep repeating this,
you can miss many times,
using up your resources
and time.

You can, however, pick up a handful of pebbles
and throw them all together,
easily bombarding your target
instantly.

DAILY DEFLECTION – QUESTIONS

1. What targets are you trying to hit – at work, at home, in
   relationships, personally, in your health, career, future etc.?

2. Where are your pebbles?

What is a breakfast briefing?

Breakfast Briefing

Awaken slowly and gently.
Be careful
as the day stumbles clumsily
against your stories of night,
trying hard not to stand
on the delicate fragments of your dreams.

Let them dance
together,
your night and day,
looking strangely at each other,
finding a place with each other,
for these fleeting moments.

Hover between your conscious
and subconscious
with due reverence
for glimpses of your unknown.
Let this unseen world
unfold its magic.

For the day
will soon be here
and the possibilities of night
may be gone forever.
In the moment,
let them play together.

DAILY DEFLECTION – QUESTIONS

1. What glimpses have you had of your unknown?

2. How might you capture and treasure the fragments of your dreams?

What will I work on today?

The Big Project

What's your big project?
What's the overall plan
that is going to deliver
what you really want?

Why are you messing about
with minor stuff, with tasks
that take up your time
and don't really matter?

Work on your big project, today
and every day.
Move it forward piece by piece.
Make it happen.

DAILY DEFLECTION – QUESTIONS

1. What is the big project that you really want to do?

2. What steps are you taking to make your big project a reality?

3. How can you prioritise your time and energy towards your big project, rather than getting bogged down in minor tasks?

Is your glass half-full?

_____

Science-Based

My three-year-old granddaughter
explained to me
that the glass isn't
half-full or
half-empty.

It's all full.
Half-full of water
and half-full of air.
Sometimes we don't see
the full picture.

DAILY DEFLECTION – QUESTIONS

1. What's in your glass?

2. What are the visible and invisible parts of your life?

What is your fog?

Mental Health

The fog has arrived.
It has stopped all traffic
in and out.

The internal systems
cannot function,
stuck in neutral.

Life goes on.
Maintenance tasks get done,
nothing else.

All communication
has ceased.
Nothing is there.

The fog usually disperses
in a day.
This is taking longer.

Two days on,
all is gridlocked.
Maybe tomorrow.

DAILY DEFLECTION – QUESTIONS

1. What is your fog?

2. What impact does it have on you?

3. When and how does your fog clear?

Are you still photocopying?

Photocopying

To make money, just copy
someone else's product or business.
I'm sure you can make it
cheaper or improve it.

Add a new feature,
make it faster,
quicker-acting
or longer-lasting.

But to change lives
and change the world,
create your own solution.
Are you still photocopying?

DAILY DEFLECTION – QUESTIONS

1. How much of what you do is photocopying?

2. What is your idea to make things better in our world or to help others?

3. What's the first step?

What is out-of-the-box thinking?

Diversifying

Networking with flowers
Growing rainbows
Building waves
Talking to carrots
Waiting on seahorses
Holding time
Investing in mornings
Collecting clouds

DAILY DEFLECTION – QUESTIONS

1. Can you escape from your normal thinking and behaviour?

2. Can you create totally out-of-the-box concepts that bring you into a new space?

What is between death and life?

Waiting Room

It's a strange place.
Sitting alone in this waiting room,
wondering when the train will arrive.
Indeed, if it will arrive
and if it will stop here.

I am stuck here, helpless
between Good Friday and Easter Sunday
on this silent Saturday, sitting and waiting.
Between death and life.
Between this world and eternity.

DAILY DEFLECTION – QUESTIONS

Waiting rooms are interesting places. They hold us for a time,
between where we were and where we are going.

1. Where are you on your journey?

2. What are you waiting on at this moment?

*This was written on Holy Saturday (between Good Friday and
Easter Sunday)*

What are the six gifts of Self?

Looking After Ourselves

We can only be kind
if we are kind
to ourselves first.

We can only be generous
if we are generous
to ourselves first.

We can only be loved
if we love
ourselves first.

We can only be compassionate
if we are compassionate
to ourselves first.

We can only be gentle
if we are gentle
to ourselves first.

We can only be merciful
if we show mercy
to ourselves first.

DAILY DEFLECTION – QUESTIONS

1. Are you sometimes too hard on yourself? When? Why?

2. How might you work on being more forgiving and understanding towards yourself?

3. How can being kind, generous, and compassionate towards yourself ultimately benefit your relationships with others?

Retreat 2 – Notes and Key Points

Day 1

_____

_____

_____

Day 2

_____

_____

_____

Day 3

_____

_____

_____

Day 4

_____

_____

_____

Day 5

_____

_____

_____

Day 6

_____

_____

_____

Day 7

_____

_____

_____

Overall thoughts about the week

_____

_____

_____

_____

Points to take with me on the journey

_____

_____

_____

_____

Personal Development Retreat

3

When does the sun rise?

Battery Life

Each morning without fail
the sun rises on the horizon,
slowly emerging into full view,
so bright that I cannot look for long.

Each morning without fail
the sun rises on the horizon,
whatever the circumstances,
whatever I'm doing.

Each morning without fail
the sun rises on the horizon.
Before I was here and after I am gone,
the sun rises on the horizon.

DAILY DEFLECTION – QUESTIONS

1. Will you make a plan to sit and watch a sunrise? Take a journal (and camera) with you.

2. Write down your thoughts and impressions once you've done this.

What's in your rucksack?

The Window

For years my friend carried
a huge bag of stones
in a rucksack on his back.
The pain of the past
was with him
in every step he took.

One day he noticed
a window in his house
that he had never seen before.
It was a small window,
some eight feet
from the ground.

It was impossible
to jump up
and look through the window,
for the stones, as always,
weighed so heavily.
So, he just sat there.

Then, he opened his rucksack
and, taking out the stones,
he placed them
one by one
on top of each other,
to create a set of steps.

He got rid of his burden.
He gained a new perspective.
And now, each day
he steps up,
and looks out
of his window.

DAILY DEFLECTION – QUESTIONS

1. Is there a rucksack that you have been carrying for many years that is perhaps full of regret, loss, disappointment, a broken relationship or memories of a difficult time?

2. What and where is your window?

3. How might you unpack your rucksack?

What does Leapfrog mean for us?

Leap Year

The core personal development question is,
'What am I really capable of?'
The response isn't
about business, work or money.

It's about who we are,
and looking beyond our perceived limitations.
It's about growing into our capacity,
even if we cannot perceive it fully.

This is the search for something
we never thought we would look at
even though, deep down,
we know we have the potential.

This is the leapfrog.
It's not linear, cumulative or predictable.
It's about us leaving our lily pad
and just going.

DAILY DEFLECTION – QUESTIONS

1. What are you really capable of?

2. What have you never thought you could do?

3. What does your new lily pad look like?

What is the generational shift?

Takeover

It's that point in life
when the younger generation
take over the reins.

It's a specific incident or situation
where they step up
to assist us or sort out something.

And we think,
This is it.
This is the moment of takeover.

And we smile
with gratitude for their help,
and for them.

DAILY DEFLECTION – QUESTIONS

1. What emotions might you experience when you realise that the younger generation is taking over what you used to do?

2. How can you prepare for a time when you are no longer able to do all that you used to?

3. How can you help those you might soon be taking over from?

What is our operating system?

Operating System

Spirituality is not something airy-fairy.
It is simply the way that we give meaning
to all that we are and all that we do.
It is the fabric of who we are.

Spirituality isn't outside of us
or detached from us.
It is our operating system,
silently working away.

DAILY DEFLECTION – QUESTIONS

1. How would you define your operating system?

2. What keeps you going?

3. How often do you check, service or update your operating system?

How can we create a new recipe?

Outside Catering

The boss-employee relationship
is deeply flawed.
It is not a true construct
for it restricts both parties.

We can only bring a fixed menu
to the job table,
providing the same meals every day
in every workplace.

We all leave behind
kitchens full of food,
unused equipment
and recipe books unopened.

DAILY DEFLECTION – QUESTIONS

1. Can you list all of the skills, experience, interests and knowledge that you leave at home when you go to work?

2. What new recipe might you create today?

3. How will you build your Outside Catering business?

Is faith the same as love?

Multi-Faith

You do not need to have faith
to fulfil your purpose.
You do not need to have any religion
to fulfil your purpose.

Your purpose is love.
For love is our faith and our religion,
unique in each of us, in all that we are
and in all that we are here to do.

DAILY DEFLECTION – QUESTIONS

1. Write down your personal definitions for each of the following
   three words: *faith*, *religion* and *love*.

2. Are there any connections or overlaps in your definitions?

How can I get more business?

Key Worker

Are you looking for more clients,
slowly building your email list
or trying to learn online marketing?

Are you promoting yourself or your business?
Do you use Facebook or Instagram and do all the 'stuff'
you hear so much about on the internet?

Are you being sucked into apps or websites
that promise amazing opportunities
but cost you money?

Have you been on training courses
or webinars that always
end up selling to you?

You can spend a fortune on other people's products,
trying to earn more money
to build your future.

You can waste your precious time
chasing activities and learning the latest things
that just don't count.

Do what you should be doing.
Follow your own path
and use your skills to help others.

DAILY DEFLECTION – QUESTIONS

1. How would you describe your path?

2. How can you use your skills and experience in more and new ways to help others?

What is a personal stocktake?

Stocktake

My *display until* date is Thursday.
My *best before* date is Friday.
My *use by* date is Saturday.
My *recycling* date is Sunday.

When should I take stock?

DAILY DEFLECTION – QUESTIONS

1. What are you including in your next personal stocktake?

2. What are you measuring and counting?

3. How often do you need to stocktake?

What is inclusion?

Inclusion

Inclusion is made real
through the rain
watering all of our crops,
wherever they may be.
No preconditions,
no preferences,
reliably and consistently.

Inclusion is made real
through the sunshine
warming all of us,
wherever we may be.
No preconditions,
no preferences,
reliably and consistently.

Inclusion is made real
through each of us
reaching out to others,
wherever they may be.
No preconditions,
no preferences,
reliably and consistently.

DAILY DEFLECTION – QUESTIONS

1. Does your Inclusion Policy at work focus on everyone, or only certain categories of people? How might you begin to change this?

2. On a personal level, who are you reaching out to?

Retreat 3 – Notes and Key Points

Day 1

_____

_____

_____

Day 2

_____

_____

_____

Day 3

_____

_____

_____

Day 4

_____

_____

_____

Day 5

_____

_____

_____

Day 6

_____

_____

_____

Day 7

_____

_____

_____

Overall thoughts about the week

_____

_____

_____

_____

Points to take with me on the journey

_____

_____

_____

_____

Personal Development Retreat

4

What is a personal needs analysis?

Needs Analysis

Sometimes there is
no need to think,
no need to speak,
no need to act.

Sometimes we
just need to stop,
just need to sit,
just need to be.

DAILY DEFLECTION – QUESTIONS

1. Can you find a quiet place with no distractions? Sit down and relax. Try and empty your brain of all thoughts. Deliberately leave a space of nothingness. Keep coming back to this emptiness. Just be.

2. At the finish time, write down what happened and what you've learned.

3. Repeat the above process every day for five days.

What do we mean by give and take?

Give and Take

In the world of want, I strive for more:
more income, a bigger house or a better job,
recognition, popularity or a sense of importance.

In the world of plenty, I have more than I need.
From this place I can reach out to you,
free to share all that I have and all that I am.

DAILY DEFLECTION – QUESTIONS

1. List five situations where you have been in the world of want.

2. List five situations where you have been in the world of plenty.

3. What do these ten points tell you about yourself?

What is the assimilation effect?

Assimilation Effect

My perfect day is made up of
hundreds of imperfect moments.
Each one is amazing and magical
and yet, not perfect.

You see, this day isn't just a collection
of hundreds of imperfect moments,
but rather a unique composition
that makes today perfect.

It's a realisation and an understanding
that goes beyond the individual pieces of each day
and pulls together a picture
that is perfection in itself.

I go beyond a *sum of the parts* valuation.
I look beyond the moments and activities
and realise just what is happening
with me, within me and around me.

Perfect happiness exists in each of us
in all of those imperfect, day-to-day interactions
and unique moments that characterise
who and what we are.

DAILY DEFLECTION – QUESTIONS

1. Write down some of the imperfect moments of your day, taking today or yesterday as your case study. Why was each moment imperfect?

2. Now, 'flip' each of these and discover the unique moment in each interaction or activity for you.

3. How do you look back on this day in its entirety?

Why is failure important in meditation?

Meditation Masterclass

And when nothing happens,
nothing seems to work
and there is no conversation,
recognise that this is about
just sitting and just being.

There is no need for productivity.
There is no need for thought.
There is no need for inspiration.
Just sit with no expectation.
Just relax. Just be in that moment.

For our failure to meditate, or reflect,
or pray, or even sit,
takes us closer
to our greatest success.
When the world wants to drag us back,
stay with the failure.

DAILY DEFLECTION – QUESTIONS

1. Create some *me time* and just sit on your own with no thoughts or expectations.

2. Write down what happens – and remember that there is no such thing as failure or 'This doesn't work for me'.

3. Repeat this process when you can.

What is contribution?

Contribution

If we are not different,
we are just more of the same.

DAILY DEFLECTION – QUESTIONS

1. We are different to others, and we all have a different contribution to make. What is your contribution?

2. Our future life is not just more of the same. It is not just extending what has happened up to now. How will yours be different?

Can we declutter ourselves?

Declutter

Clear out your office.
Empty your cabinets
and get rid of your old papers.
Close the door behind you.

We don't have to continue doing
what we've always done.
We don't have to carry
all of our imperfect pasts with us.

We can dispose of our papers
and separate out what we no longer need.
We can start afresh
from wherever we are.

Unburden yourself from your past.
Leave boxes and bags behind.
Take only that which gives you
joy, peace and happiness.

DAILY DEFLECTION – QUESTIONS

1. Are you ready to clear out your 'office'? What do you no longer need to hold onto?

2. What is it that gives you joy, peace and happiness?

3. What does your fresh start look like?

What is your ambition?

Ambition

The main task that you're working on
at the moment is really a small thing.
Beyond this, there is a larger task
that you are easily capable of.
Just think for a moment:
What is this larger task?
For this is what you should be doing.
This should be your focus.

And beyond this larger task
is a greater task,
one of real significance,
that you are easily capable of.
Just think for a moment:
What is this greater task?
For this is what you should be doing.
This should be your focus.

And beyond this greater task
is the greatest task,
where all of your effort should be,
that you are easily capable of.
Just think for a moment:

What is this greatest task?
For this is what you should be doing.
This should be your focus.

DAILY DEFLECTION – QUESTIONS

1. What is the key task that you are working on now?

2. What is the larger task, the greater task beyond this and the greatest task?

3. What is the level of your ambition?

What is *Click and Collect* for people?

Click and Collect

Sometimes we can act like a tortoise,
moving very slowly,
step by step,
sometimes making progress,
and sometimes
standing still.

But what if we were a seagull,
kicking off from a standing start?
Zooming at great pace,
covering vast distances,
deciding where to land
and immediately placing ourselves there?
Let's redesign our delivery.

DAILY DEFLECTION – QUESTIONS

1. What is your starting point?

2. Where do you want to go?

3. Now think like a seagull – and create a new route.

Can we have a vision without clarity?

Vision

When I take off my glasses
everything becomes unclear,
for there is no clarity.

Everything is a blur,
with shade and forms merging
into one another,

and as night approaches,
streetlights create a
forest of bright trees.

It is a landscape
without definition.
For there is no clarity.

And yet, this lack of definition
creates a totality and a oneness
that is at ease with itself.

Take off your glasses
and you will see more clearly
where there is no clarity.

DAILY DEFLECTION – QUESTIONS

1. What is your vision? What do you want to see happen in your life?

2. Can you step away from your normal thought process for a moment? *(Take your glasses off if you wear them.)*

3. Without this usual perspective, in this lack of clarity, what do you see? Keep looking.

Where is eternity?

Thinking Outside the Box

Imagine if we go through this time
not asking the *real questions*.
What if our focus is solely
on present events?

Do we not realise
that there was a time
when we were not here?
An eternity before we existed.

And do we not realise
that there will be a time
when we will not be here?
An eternity still to come.

DAILY DEFLECTION – QUESTIONS

1. Look beyond present events and list the *real questions* for you.

2. How are you planning to find the answers?

Retreat 4 – Notes and Key Points

Day 1

_____

_____

_____

Day 2

_____

_____

_____

Day 3

_____

_____

_____

Day 4

_____

_____

_____

Day 5

_____

_____

_____

Day 6

_____

_____

_____

Day 7

_____

_____

_____

Overall thoughts about the week

_____

_____

_____

_____

Points to take with me on the journey

_____

_____

_____

_____

Personal Development Retreat

5

How can we use one minute of mindfulness?

Instant Loans

Lend your love today
to someone far away
in another country
who is struggling,
with no basic resources
or help for their family,
and who can see no future.

Connect with them now
for just one minute.
Reach out to them
at a personal level
as their father or mother,
as their son or daughter,
in our family of one.

Think of them now.
For this will become
the greatest thing
that you ever do,
changing everything
in an instant.
Lend your love today.

DAILY DEFLECTION – QUESTIONS

1. In this one minute of mindfulness, see if you can connect beyond all geography to be with someone who desperately needs help. Sit quietly and be one with them.

2. How can we lend our love to those in need, even if we are physically far away?

3. How can we shift our perspective to see the global community as our family of one?

What is your different future?

Rewind

Let us not go back to how it was.
Let us not go back to our old way.
For our future is forwards –
not backwards.
Let us not repeat it all again
for we will never be the same again.

New ways of working,
new ways of communicating,
new ways of living,
new ways of thinking
and a different way of being
are now part of each of us.

When we step out through the door
we can plan a different future.
And then, when we look back,
we will see that this was the moment
when we changed.
The moment we changed everything.

DAILY DEFLECTION - QUESTIONS

1. How have you changed over the last 42 days?

2. What is different about the way you work, communicate, live and think about everything?

3. What is your different future?

What is blockchain kindness?

Blockchain

With blocks of information
being passed digitally
from person to person,
we can track every
financial transaction in the chain.
We can always go right back
to the source,
the first block in the chain.

Likewise, every time we reach out
to help someone,
we begin to build a chain
from person to person
that spreads forever.
We create blockchains of kindness.
We are the source,
the first block in the chain.

DAILY DEFLECTION – QUESTIONS

1. Think of one person you could help today. As a result of your input, what might they do, or do better?

2. Each of us encounters hundreds of blockchain kindness opportunities (BKO) every day. Some are as simple as saying thank you, sending a text or offering some advice. Starting from now, list the next ten BKOs you see today.

How can I increase my response rate?

Response Rate

When I shake the little tree,
every single leaf responds.
Instantly, hundreds of leaves
all wave back to me.
They shimmer enthusiastically as one,
each in their own unique way.

DAILY DEFLECTION – QUESTIONS

1. What tree will you shake today?

2. What are you responding to, enthusiastically with others, as one?

Retreat 5:5

Are you pleased with your current workload?

Workload

Be thankful for the tasks
you have to do today.
For there will come a time
when those seeking your help
or needing your input
will no longer be asking.
There will come a time
when you will not be able to help.

DAILY DEFLECTION – QUESTIONS

1. What are your priority tasks today?

2. Can you look beyond the activity to further explore the relationships involved in each task?

What is your spiritual challenge?

Road Works

There is a blockage,
a huge boulder on the road
right in front of me.

I've been looking at it for years.
I'm now right up against it
and I must decide what to do:

to continue standing here looking
at the boulder in the road,
or to move it.

What's on the other side
of this boulder in the road?
Where does this road lead?

So, this is not a physical challenge,
for I would have moved
the boulder in the road years ago.

It's a spiritual challenge.
It's one of becoming and being.
It's my boulder in the road.

DAILY DEFLECTION - QUESTIONS

1. What is your spiritual challenge?

2. How will you move this boulder in the road?

3 Where are you on your journey of becoming and being?

What will you harvest from today?

Harvest

Every conversation is a story.
Every person we meet is a case study.
Every situation offers options.
Every thought can open a new door.
Every job teaches us new skills.
Every task produces opportunities.
Every memory holds real treasure,
for we grow through all things.

Every moment holds an asset for us,
enabling us to make sense of life,
helping us with a different perspective
and to find our best way.
So, do not forget your stories.
Write down your case studies,
explore all of your options and open new doors.
Harvest all that you are today.

DAILY DEFLECTION – QUESTIONS

1. Start to collect all your experience, notes, writings, reports, ideas and stories together into relevant folders. Begin to build your *harvest* files and folders on your computer or laptop.

2. What will you harvest from yesterday and today?

3. Devote some time to harvesting every day. Look at what is emerging for you.

What is the reality of completeness?

Complete Works

We only have one version of the story.
We can only define what we see as reality
from our perspective.
We view everything
through our personal filters.

Others too have their version of the story.
Each person tries to make sense of life
through their personal filter.
Billions of realities across the world,
and all different.

And beyond all of this
is the reality of completeness.
This sees and links everything
and everyone as we truly are:
the complete works.

DAILY DEFLECTION – QUESTIONS

1. Think of three people you know or work with. In a sentence, describe how they each see you.

2. Where and how do these views differ from how you picture yourself?

What do you own?

Ownership

There is no such thing as 'mine'.
It is there for all of us.
For as soon as we claim
something for ourselves,
we lessen its potential
and we limit our capacity for growth.

Let us shift from ownership and self
to potential and possibilities.
Let us leave all in that sacred space
that we cannot own,
so that through sharing and service,
we become all that we should be.

DAILY DEFLECTION – QUESTIONS

1. What do you own?

2. What are you holding onto that in some way may limit you?

What are your areas of unknowing?

Behaviour Modification

Deep programming, social conditioning and learned behaviours
cause us to think this way or behave in that way.
We have learned what works for us and what doesn't.
It is easy to see why we continue to confine our thinking
to that which we know or are used to.

Our current levels of understanding and routine behaviour
have hidden other routes and areas of unknowing.
What should we be doing that we haven't even thought of?
We need to find a way through, around,
above or beyond our knowledge base.

Perhaps we need to go deeper than our normal dialogue.
Perhaps we need new conversations, perspectives and insights.
For this time is about making connections
with pieces that we may not know,
to deliver a dream that we would never have imagined.

DAILY DEFLECTION – QUESTIONS

1. What are your areas of unknowing?

2. What new connections might you explore that you have never even thought of before?

3. What is the dream that you have never imagined?

Retreat 5 – Notes and Key Points

Day 1

_____

_____

_____

Day 2

_____

_____

_____

Day 3

_____

_____

_____

Day 4

_____

_____

_____

Day 5

_____

_____

_____

Day 6

_____

_____

_____

Day 7

_____

_____

_____

Overall thoughts about the week

_____

_____

_____

_____

Points to take with me on the journey

_____

_____

_____

_____

Personal Development Retreat

6

How visible is your determination to others?

Determination

Early this morning as I sat in the woods,
I spotted a young woman jogging in all her gear.
She was pushing her pram and baby
in front of her as she ran,
maintaining a steady pace.
I thought to myself, *What determination!*

About ten minutes later, she approached
where I was sitting and reading.
I looked up and said,
'I think you're marvellous, absolutely amazing!'
She looked at me, laughed and replied, 'Thank you!'
without changing her pace.

Sometimes when we try
to get across the true meaning of a word,
the definition is not enough
and an image can perhaps capture it better.
Determination, for me, will always be
a young woman running with her pram.

DAILY DEFLECTION – QUESTIONS

1. What does determination mean to you? What's your image?

2. How is your determination made real and visible each day?

What is your message?

Messenger

When you were born
you were given
a message for the world.

As you live your life
you will uncover and understand
this message.

And then, for the rest of your life,
you must share your
message with the world.

DAILY DEFLECTION – QUESTIONS

1. How much of your message have you uncovered?

2. Write down what you understand and what you have yet to make sense of.

3. Your message, however incomplete, is your purpose. Be brave and true to yourself. How can you share who you really are today?

What is your rate of return?

Yield

Give way.
Let others win.
Operate at a higher level.

Give way.
Let it all pass you by.
Stay detached in your own place.

Give way.
Let your rate of return
be what cannot be measured.

DAILY DEFLECTION – QUESTIONS

1. What are you trying to win?

2. Who are you competing with, at work or at home?

3. How do you measure your yield – your rate of return?

What are the nine principles of cause and effect?

Cause and Effect

If you move sideways,
you'll get a better view.

If you take a few steps back,
you'll make bigger jumps.

If you need to stop for breath,
you've already gone too far.

If you laugh and smile,
you'll learn to enjoy yourself.

If you feed someone,
you'll not go hungry.

If you stop and plan your route,
you won't go around in circles.

If you are tired,
you can rest.

If you close your eyes,
you'll see more clearly.

If you can sit in silence,
you'll hear the answer.

DAILY DEFLECTION – QUESTIONS

1. Which of the above nine statements holds the most meaning to you at the moment?

2. How will you act on this?

Why is being lost so important?

Lost

We tend to think of being lost
as a negative thing. It seems to indicate
that we've gone off our path,
gone astray or lost our way,
or are not where we should be.

But perhaps the opposite is true.
Perhaps being lost is an opportunity
to find a different way,
to be in a different place,
or to explore something new.

I remember on holiday when I was young,
my mum sitting with a map on her knee,
my dad always driving 'too fast' and missing
the right turns. He would never go back!
He would always find a new way.

So, can we deliberately choose to be lost?
Can we step out of our predictability
and discover an unfamiliar route?
Can we put ourselves in situations
that lead to a different set of outcomes?

DAILY DEFLECTION – QUESTIONS

1. In what way has your life become predictable? In what areas are you yearning for something different?

2. How might you step out of 'more of the same'? How could you take a different way and get lost?

What is the best way to clean up a mess?

Kitchen Roll

Absorbing is the gift
of embracing everything,
taking it all in,
and cherishing
how this changes us forever.

DAILY DEFLECTION – QUESTIONS

1. In what ways might you use mindfulness, walking or sitting quietly to become better at absorbing and embracing life experiences?

2. Can you explain how you have learnt to embrace the messiness of life and to take it all in?

3. How do you make sure that absorbing life experiences helps you to grow and change for the better?

What is a pilgrim?

Leadership

Leadership is not about changing roles
or shifting direction.
It is not about team development
or business strategy.

Leadership is a fundamental shift
in our being – what we are, how we think,
the priorities we set
and how we behave.

Leadership is a behavioural,
emotional and spiritual process.
It's rewiring the hard disk of our being
for a completely different output.

We are no longer
mass-market products
of the consumer age,
but pilgrims with a purpose.

DAILY DEFLECTION – QUESTIONS

1. What does it mean to be a pilgrim with a purpose?

2. What are your outputs?

3. How can you rewire your being for a different type of leadership?

Where are you hiding?

Hide and Seek

Come out from under your duvet.
We need to see you.
It's a beautiful sunny morning.
We need to hear from you.

Come out from yourself.
We need you to be with us.
It's your day to shine.
We need you to help us.

DAILY DEFLECTION – QUESTIONS

1. How have you been hiding recently?

2. How will you shine today?

How can we build a better world?

Building Services

There are people looking to build
a better world.
They're looking beyond
business models and technology.
They're looking at the development
of a collective approach
with a collaboration of ideas and support
defined by service.

This is a different model and way
outside of the business box.
It is defining what we are about
in a different way.
It is about setting
different expectations of ourselves,
proactively supporting those we know
and those we do not know.

DAILY DEFLECTION – QUESTIONS

1. What is your model for working with others?

2. How are you proactively working with others to build a better world?

Where do we truly belong?

Resilience

We spend all our lives doing stuff.
Then planning and doing more stuff.
It's exhausting.

Our life is passing us by.
And still we plan
and do more stuff.

Schedules, routines and to-do lists.
They strap us into
this world of doing,
like chains.
We accept this as normal
and yet, it doesn't have to be like this.
We can get off the treadmill.

Step back from the world of doing
and see a different place:
the world of being.

Here, all is calm and peaceful.
There are no timetables
and no demands.

It's a timeless place
that holds all that is important to us.
Yet many of us rarely go there.

Get off the treadmill every now and then.
You will immediately arrive at the world of being,
with its peace and gentleness, and with nothing to do.

Just be. Be yourself.
Let love fill you and renew you
for the next part of your doing journey.

This is the font of resilience.
The origin of all.
This is where we can all be truly ourselves.
It is our place of being, where we truly belong.

DAILY DEFLECTION – QUESTIONS

1. What is the stuff that can trap or exhaust you at times?

2. When will you step back and take a little time to refresh yourself at your font of resilience?

Retreat 6 – Notes and Key Points

Day 1

_____

_____

_____

Day 2

_____

_____

_____

Day 3

_____

_____

_____

Day 4

_____

_____

_____

Day 5

_____

_____

_____

Day 6

_____

_____

_____

Day 7

_____

_____

_____

Overall thoughts about the week

_____

_____

_____

_____

Points to take with me on the journey

_____

_____

_____

_____

Personal Development Retreat

7

What is our disciplinary hearing?

Disciplinary Hearing

You must never lose
your battle cry
or your willingness to go for it.

You must never dilute
what you once dreamt about,
what you saw so clearly.

You must never give up,
no matter what happens,
no matter what others may say.

DAILY DEFLECTION – QUESTIONS

1. What did you once see so clearly?

2. How can you discover (or rediscover) your battle cry?

What is our lifetime guarantee?

Lifetime Guarantee

We are all made of pure love.
The same pure love is present
in each of us
and unites us all together.

Our lives add a rough crust
of worldliness
over this pure love,
hiding who and what we truly are.

Life's circumstances, difficulties
and personal choices
can add layer upon layer,
burying our real selves.

But underneath it all,
no matter what we do,
exists our pure love,
secure and untarnished.

And so it is that each of us,
and all together,
can be protected
and cared for, forever.

DAILY DEFLECTION – QUESTIONS

1. What does your rough crust of worldliness look like?

2. What life circumstances, difficulties and personal choices have contributed to hiding your real self?

What is a good morning thank-you?

Coffee Morning

I just love this first cup of coffee
in the morning.
It's my moment of appreciation
for the day I've been given.

It's my celebration and gratitude
for a new start
full of wonder of all that will unfold
before me and for me.

I gently leave to one side
the troubles from yesterday.
I do not carry
the worries of the past.

I begin afresh,
right here, right now,
with both hands clasped in thanks
around this first cup of coffee.

DAILY DEFLECTION – QUESTIONS

1. How do you welcome and say thanks for each new day that you have been given? It can be as simple as a thoughtful cup of coffee!

2. What does your start to a new day consist of?

What is self-actualisation?

Self-Actualisation

Mission and purpose ask us
to reach into ourselves
and try to understand
who we are, why we are here
and what we are meant to do at this time.

Self-actualisation is made real
and visible for us every day
through this ongoing inward search
and the ever-present uncovering
of truth on our lifelong journey.

DAILY DEFLECTION – QUESTIONS

1. What is your mission and purpose?

2. What have you uncovered today about yourself?

How can we manage complex projects easily?

The Whole Shebang

When you're trying to build
a framework or a model
that includes everything...

When you're trying to juggle
all the tasks and activities
to make the project work...

When you're looking at
the implications of what could happen
two years down the line...

When you're trying to take
everybody else's perspective
and feelings into account...

When you're looking to make
things better and explore
all the possibilities...

This is the whole shebang of
inclusion, when you're dealing
with everyone and everything together.

DAILY DEFLECTION – QUESTIONS

1. How do you approach decision-making and project management when trying to take all perspectives and possibilities into account?

2. In what ways can the concept of *the whole shebang* be applied to personal development, home life, career development and business success?

What do we mean by *hands-on*?

Hands-On

I can remember you
washing your hands in the kitchen sink.
You'd just come home from work
with garage grease up to your elbows.
And Ma rescued the situation with a towel
whilst serving us our tea.

I can remember you
asking me to hold out my hands
so that you could wind the wool into balls.
And you'd sit at night
knitting Aran jumpers
that were admired by all.

DAILY DEFLECTION – QUESTIONS

1. Being hands-on means that we are actively involved. We make things happen with others. What are you making happen at the moment?

2. What hands-on activities do you have with your partner, friends and/or children in the daily activities of life?

3. How are you working with others who are holding out their hands, asking for help?

How do we address exclusion?

Exclusion

It is no longer enough
to stand inside
the tent and
call people to join you.

Sometimes we need to go
outside the tent and
work with people
so that we can all walk in together.

DAILY DEFLECTION – QUESTIONS

1. Who is in your tent?

2. How can I or others join you?

What is net gain?

Net Gain

If you pull back the net curtain,
you will see clearly.
You will see forever
into the distance.

If you don't pull back the net curtain,
all you will see is
the net curtain
and a vague light behind it.

DAILY DEFLECTION – QUESTIONS

1. What would you like to see more clearly?

2. What is the net curtain?

How are we all connected to everything?

Connections

I know that I am nothing
but that I am connected
to everything through love.

I know that I can do so little
but through this great love
I can do everything.

I therefore give myself to love
so that everyone can be well
and all as it should be.

In submitting to infinite goodness
I unleash a gentle power within me
beyond all imagining.

For it is in this complete submission
that I am connected to everything
that ever was and is yet to come.

DAILY DEFLECTION – QUESTIONS

1. What are you connected to?

2. Who are you connected to?

What is a privilege?

Honours List

I worry about what has happened,
forgetting that all is a privilege.
I regret the mess I've made,
forgetting that all is a privilege.
I feel disappointed by what I've done,
forgetting that all is a privilege.

Each day brings an ongoing torrent
of privileges, opportunities and gifts.
Irrespective of how well I manage these,
the torrent continues.
And so, as I try to embrace what happens today,
I remember that all is a privilege.

DAILY DEFLECTION – QUESTIONS

1. What privileges, opportunities and gifts have you already
   received today?

2. How will you embrace and use these?

Retreat 7 – Notes and Key Points

Day 1

_____

_____

_____

Day 2

_____

_____

_____

Day 3

_____

_____

_____

Day 4

_____

_____

_____

Day 5

_____

_____

_____

Day 6

_____

_____

_____

Day 7

_____

_____

_____

Overall thoughts about the week

_____

_____

_____

_____

Points to take with me on the journey

_____

_____

_____

_____

Personal Development Retreat

8

What is the real stuff?

Priorities

I've run out of time.
I tick the boxes,
get halfway through,
but the end of the list
never gets done.
I just don't have the time.

I start afresh each day.
I rewrite my list
and put my priorities at the top.
But the important tasks
never get done.
I run out of time.

It's the same routine
as I set out the tasks.
And then it hits me
that the real stuff never
even gets onto my list;
never gets done.

DAILY DEFLECTION – QUESTIONS

1. What is the *real stuff* for you?

2. How will you rethink and reorganise your day to get the real stuff done?

What is the gift of grace?

Trial and Error

My failures remind me
that I am still on the right path.
They point me again
in the right direction.
They encourage me
as I start again.

This is not about
determination or effort.
Rather, it is about
the gift of grace,
which opens the window
to let the light in.

DAILY DEFLECTION – QUESTIONS

1. What are your failures?

2. How would you describe the gift of grace that enables you to start again?

What is the prison of expectation?

The Gift of Freedom

Throw open the windows.
Kick open the doors.
Let the sunshine in.

It's been dull and dreary here for too long.
It's sapped your energy
and killed your enthusiasm.

Escape from the prison
of expectation, routine
and just getting by.

All is there before you,
waiting expectantly.
And now you are free.

Go to new places.
Meet everyone who needs you,
and work with them to make a difference.

Explode now with warmth.
Do everything you should.
Do all that you can.

DAILY DEFLECTION – QUESTIONS

1. How will you escape from the prison of expectation, routine and just getting by?

2. What will you do with this new freedom?

What is the top investment strategy?

Investment Strategy

When we speak of investment,
we think of the financial return on our money.
But this is not investment;
this is just making more money – or trying to.

If we really want a return on our resources
then we should invest in the skills, experience,
knowledge and passion of all the people
we know, and those we don't know.

And we don't do this for financial gain.
We do it because we have money
and because we can help them
to become what they should be.

This is the real investment:
helping people to be all that they can be
and, in turn, enabling us to be
who we should be.

When we die, we will have no money.
We can't take it with us.
So, plan to invest all you can while you can
and watch the fruits grow while you're still here.

Create ripples of goodness.
Plant seeds of hope.
Invest in all that is positive and kind.
Make your mark on all those you meet.

Invest your time helping others.
Go way beyond duty or expectation.
Surprise others with your commitment,
your energy, your enthusiasm and your spirit.

DAILY DEFLECTION – QUESTIONS

1. Who is your investment strategy focused on?

2. What is the return on your resources?

Are we semi-detached?

Semi-Detached

It's obvious to all of us
how the tasks, worries
and responsibilities of daily life
can wear us down.

We also know from experience
that these all pass in due course,
but still, we get overcome at times
with the demands upon us.

It is in the quieter moments,
when life is less hectic,
that we appreciate the peace
and gentleness that lies beneath everything.

This is where we really belong.
And so, our daily focus must be
to stay semi-detached, and balance
being busy in our world, yet quiet in ourselves.

DAILY DEFLECTION – QUESTIONS

1. What are the tasks and worries of daily life that can wear you down?

2. When and where do you have your quieter moments?

3. Can you make time each day to stay semi-detached?

What are your daily reminders?

Reminders

Never too old,
never too tired,
never too late,
never too much trouble.

Always enough,
always great,
always yes,
always love.

DAILY DEFLECTION – QUESTIONS

1. Write another two phrases beginning with *never*.

2. Write another two phrases beginning with *always*.

Is God an inclusion manager?

Inclusion Manager

God has a different relationship
with every single person.
God communicates with us
and works with each of us in different ways.

We all have different roles and each role
is equal, vital, personal and unique.
The unbeliever and the monk:
we all share the same space.

DAILY DEFLECTION – QUESTIONS

1. If *Inclusion Manager* is another name for God, how is your role
   equal, vital, personal and unique?

2. What is this same space that we all share?

What are the eight tasks of life?

Multi-Tasking

Our task is to continually
seek the truth,
not just to listen to others
or be influenced by popular opinion.

Our task is to listen
to what is deep within us,
not to follow the crowd
or miss the real conversations.

Our task is to live
the life given to us
in full, without reservation, without excuses,
without blinkers, each day.

Our task is to become
all that we should be,
to be our own person, there for others,
the helper and peace-builder.

Our task is to uncover and use
our gifts and skills to help others,
not to build wealth
or to become important.

Our task is to set our own course
and not to be buffeted
by events and activities around us,
or by what pleases others.

Our task is to reach out
to all others, especially those who are hungry
and those who ask for our help,
in any way, today.

Our task is to love,
to be a source of encouragement
and a guide, so that we all may become
what we can be.

DAILY DEFLECTION – QUESTIONS

1. Go through each of the eight tasks above and make a note for your to-do list this week.

2. Which of the above tasks holds the most potential for you?

What does *time and motion* mean for us?

Time and Motion

Grasp every moment.
Waste not one second.
Fill each minute with joy
and gratitude.

Seize opportunities.
Show your enthusiasm.
Excite others.
Pass on your love.

Surprise people.
Make them smile.
Waste not one second.
Grasp every moment.

DAILY DEFLECTION – QUESTIONS

1. Time and motion studies help us to evaluate how effective we are. A day contains over 80,000 seconds. How did you do yesterday?

2. Did you seize opportunities, show your enthusiasm, excite others, pass on your love, surprise people and make them smile?

Do you have a morning business meeting with God?

Mentor

I'm not very good at the meditation thing,
so for me, it's a morning business meeting with God.
We chat through priorities and tasks.

We look at the current focus
in line with the overall strategy,
and identify people we need to talk to.

We come up with a few good ideas together,
and set out a detailed plan for the day.
We all need a mentor.

DAILY DEFLECTION – QUESTIONS

1. Who is your mentor?

2. Who do you mentor?

Retreat 8 – Notes and Key Points

Day 1

_____

_____

_____

Day 2

_____

_____

_____

Day 3

_____

_____

_____

Day 4

_____

_____

_____

Day 5

_____

_____

_____

Day 6

_____

_____

_____

Day 7

_____

_____

_____

Overall thoughts about the week

_____

_____

_____

_____

Points to take with me on the journey

_____

_____

_____

_____

Personal Development Retreat

9

How can we let go of our anger?

Peace Talks

She gently reminds me that
any fool can fall out with someone.
But I feel really angry,
betrayed and let down.
She explains that the reality is that
we are still connected,
no matter what happens.

It may seem like
the end of the road,
but before your angry outburst,
that long legal case begins
or that explosive email is sent,
just remember that this is not
the end of your story together.

For you will connect again,
sooner than you think.
So, always part on good terms.
Think well of the other,
no matter what,
for both of you are forever
part of each other's journey.

Let the anger go and be at peace
with yourself and others.
Speak well of those who let you down,
for in time they will have
no answer to your kindness
but kindness itself.
Any fool can fall out.

DAILY DEFLECTION – QUESTIONS

1. Who is it that you do not always think well of or speak well of?

2. If you were your own life coach, how would you help yourself to let go of this anger?

What's the best way to rearrange my furniture?

Interior Design

I'm using this time
as an opportunity to rethink where I am
and to start afresh.

I even moved
all my office furniture around yesterday
and it made a huge difference.

You see, I'm now able
to look out of the window at the trees
and not stare at the wall.

Moving the furniture around
has literally changed how I see things.
It's my interior design process.

DAILY DEFLECTION – QUESTIONS

1. How could you rearrange your furniture for a different perspective?
2. How could you rearrange your day for a different set of outcomes?

How would you describe 'your way'?

Scenario Planning

There are many ways.
You have your own way.
And your way has
many options and possibilities.

Stay on your own path.
It may be muddled or uncertain now
but it will become clear.
Be yourself.

Stay true to yourself
and to all those who love (and have loved) you,
for they too are on the path
of love and uncertainty.

Love all others,
for your kindness (with a smile and a helping hand)
can be a signpost on their journey –
and yours.

You have a fixed amount of time
so use every moment to work for love.
All else will pass.
Love *is*.

DAILY DEFLECTION – QUESTIONS

1. What are your options and possibilities?

2. How would you describe your way?

What is personal merchandising?

Merchandising

Rearrange yourself.
Mix up your pieces a bit
and bring out
all the love you have.
Restock your shelves.
Let the world see
a new you, the real you.

DAILY DEFLECTION – QUESTIONS

1. What can I get in your shop?

2. What is your new merchandising plan?

What are winter fireworks?

Bookstore Creativity Session

Go to a bookstore and browse.
Check out the poetry, personal development
or business books.

Collect stories, ideas, quotes and perspectives
that challenge or excite you.
Let your sense of wonder come alive.

Let possibilities and scenarios
explode in your brain like winter fireworks.
Capture the key messages.

Next time you go shopping, join me
and let us take ten minutes together
on our Bookstore Creativity Session.

DAILY DEFLECTION – QUESTIONS

1. Pick out two or three books from your shelf or bookcase that you haven't opened for ages. Browse through and write down three or four ideas. Now play with these and think, *How can I use these ideas?*

2. Next time you go shopping, join me on my Bookstore Creativity Session.

176

What is an annual performance review?

Annual Performance Review

Your time is running out.
Another year has gone.
Your life is passing by.

It is here now:
the moment to grasp
all that is meant to be;

the whole purpose
and meaning
of your life.

Your time is running out.
Another year has gone.
Your life is passing by.

It is here now:
the moment to grasp
all that is meant to be.

DAILY DEFLECTION – QUESTIONS

1. This is the key moment in your life. What will you grasp?

2. What will you achieve by this time next year – at your next annual performance review?

Can tea bags help to predict the future?

Tea Bags

When you sit and look
into your cup of tea,
what do you see
when it is finished?

Years ago, fortune tellers
would predict our future
by looking at the pattern of the leaves
resting at the bottom of the cup.

Tea bags now mean that we
throw away our tea leaves
before we drink our tea,
leaving no clues, no predictions.

So, as you dispose
of your tea bag today,
take a moment to imagine your future
and how your story will unfold.

DAILY DEFLECTION – QUESTIONS

1. Can you imagine how your life might unfold in terms of work, relationships and all that is important to you?

2. What is the one surprise or unexpected event?

3. Write out the perfect story for your future.

What is 360-degree feedback?

360-Degree Feedback

Love is not something we have to search for.
Love is with us, beside us,
and in us always,
no matter what.

So, this journey of life is an inward one:
to be love in all we are,
and an outward one:
to love all those we meet.

DAILY DEFLECTION – QUESTIONS

1. What does your love look like – inside and out?

2. List and celebrate the top five real, practical and visible outputs of your love.

What are business drivers?

Business Drivers

'Are you the driver?'
This is the question I was asked
when paying for tea and a scone in the café
by the ancient monastic site at Clonmacnoise in Ireland.

I guess it was my solitary nature, the sunglasses
or absence of a camera that led to her question.
I was clearly not part of the Japanese tourist group.
Now, every day, I ask myself: *Are you the driver?*

DAILY DEFLECTION – QUESTIONS

1. What are the drivers in your business or work?

2. What are you driving?

What does *follow-through* mean?

Happy Father's Day

Every time I play golf,
I am with you, remembering
to keep my head down
and watch the ball.

I always want to play
on my own, partly due to
embarrassment at my standard,
but also, just to be with you.

For it is not about the score,
the lost balls, my swing, or even
the one or two good shots
that redeem the round.

It's about being with you,
treasuring the gift that you gave me,
and remembering your call
to follow through.

DAILY DEFLECTION – QUESTIONS

1. What are your best memories of those who loved you?

2. What is your follow through?

Retreat 9 – Notes and Key Points

Day 1

_____

_____

_____

Day 2

_____

_____

_____

Day 3

_____

_____

_____

Day 4

_____

_____

_____

Day 5

_____

_____

_____

Day 6

_____

_____

_____

Day 7

_____

_____

_____

Overall thoughts about the week

_____

_____

_____

_____

Points to take with me on the journey

_____

_____

_____

_____

Personal Development Retreat

10

What is a good relocation package?

Relocation Package

We're moving home next week.
My wife is busy ensuring all the lightbulbs
are working. She will clean the flat
from top to bottom. She's had new window
locks fitted as we'd lost the keys.

We've been to the hardware store
and bought a new electric fire to replace
the one that we are taking. The shop assistant
laughed, as it was the hottest summer on record!
We have even bought better-quality
ornamental coals for the gas fire.

We've touched up all the paintwork where
pictures used to hang. We've left a welcome
pack of notes with instructions on the boiler,
door key codes, internet connections,
recycling arrangements and heating controls.
The last thing will be to leave a bunch
of flowers and a bottle of wine.

We've spent all this time and we will
never see the people who move in. We will
not know who takes our place here. We will
not know if they are kind or thoughtful. We will
not know if they are younger or older than us.

When I question all this activity, I am gently
reminded that it's just about doing for others
as we would like them to do for us. She asks,
'If we were to walk in here,
what would we like to see?'

It's not so much about us leaving and moving,
but them arriving. Sometimes we need
to relocate our thinking.
For relocation is not so much about where
you go but what you leave behind.

*(Three weeks after we left, we received a
lovely thank-you card)*

DAILY DEFLECTION – QUESTIONS

1. What is your next move in life or work?

2. What will you leave behind?

What is a war of peace?

Peace-Building

Throw your grenades
of love into the world
with a quiet thought.

Fire your missiles
of help to those in need
with a wish especially for them.

Blast your kindness
to everyone you have never met
with a moment of silence for them.

Launch your propaganda offensive
with words and messages of love
and a share of your resources.

Create collateral damage
that inspires and transforms everyone
to join your war of peace.

DAILY DEFLECTION – QUESTIONS

1. What is your war of peace?

2. How can you escalate this?

What is a compass of compliance?

Compliance

To change things for the better,
you do not need to operate within
the rules of business
and the machinery of the world.
You can bypass the games of competition
and expectations of others.

You have your own compass of compliance,
your own way of being
and you are your own self.
This must grow and flourish
despite all around it,
and because of all around it.

You can set a different path,
a new way.
You can offer fresh hope
just by being totally and truthfully you.
This will create new ways of working
that will change everything – forever.

DAILY DEFLECTION – QUESTIONS

1. What guides your compass of compliance?

2. How are you changing things for the better?

What is the glass roof?

Escape Route

The bee is trapped in the conservatory,
continually bashing itself
against the glass roof
and continuously buzzing in frustration.

I open the door but he does not
change his behaviour,
what he has already learned.
He bashes away, with determination.

It's only when I reach up
with a cushion and direct him to the door,
that he finally changes his position
and makes his escape.

Our escape route is beside us,
if only we would look in a
different direction,
if only we would change our position.

DAILY DEFLECTION – QUESTIONS

1. In what situations have you repeatedly bashed yourself against a metaphorical glass roof?

2. What are the habits or behaviours that you've learned that may be keeping you trapped in your current circumstances?

3. How might you change your position or perspective to find a way out of your situation?

Will you press your reset button?

Reset Button

If we keep thinking
the same way,
we will come to the same conclusion.

If we keep doing
the same things,
we will get the same results.

If we keep looking
the same way,
we will miss what is really happening.

If we keep going in
the same direction,
we will miss the turning point.

Press your reset button.
Think differently
about everything.

DAILY DEFLECTION – QUESTIONS

1. What will happen when you press your reset button?

2. How will you think differently, do things differently, see things differently and go in a different way?

What is the future of the worldwide web?

Worldwide Web

The worldwide web has existed
since the beginning of time.
It has enabled people to link up
and help one another without limitation.

If we say a prayer today
for someone in need who we don't know,
we can reach out with love,
and we will change the world.

For our gift of love will explode
like a million meteor showers
igniting together at once,
and covering the whole world.

These explosions of love
will, in turn, create more explosions of love.
In an instant we can change,
help and support the lives of everyone.

The exponential growth of love
beyond culture, country or technology
is personal, direct and transformative.
It's our worldwide web of love.

DAILY DEFLECTION – QUESTIONS

1. Send out a message on the worldwide web of love.

2. Where will your meteor showers land?

What is the jigsaw of life?

Jigsaw Puzzle

I do not even have one piece of the jigsaw.
I don't know how many pieces there are
or what the picture is on the lid of the box.

Yet this is a jigsaw that will be completed.
For the search for pieces and the piecing together
will answer every question.

DAILY DEFLECTION – QUESTIONS

1. What pieces have you found so far?

2. What pieces are missing?

Where is your joy?

Angels

Isabella is the light of my life,
saving me from everything,
not expecting anything
and finding true joy in all things.

She helps me with mundane tasks,
bringing me to a level of understanding,
peace and real happiness
in these moments.

Her excited greeting, 'Hello, Grandad!'
makes me thankful for my years.
Her running to be lifted
makes me wish I was younger.

Isabella is my angel.

DAILY DEFLECTION – QUESTIONS

1. Who is your angel?

2. How does your angel save you?

What is your personal time zone?

Time Zone

I've changed my time zone.
I now get up at six o'clock rather than eight
and go to bed at ten o'clock rather than midnight.

By moving my time zone back two hours,
I have been able not only to redesign my day
but to reinvent the work that I do.

You see, these two amazing extra hours
every morning help me to redefine
not just the rest of the day, but who I am.

DAILY DEFLECTION – QUESTIONS

1. How could you restructure your daily routine in some way to create *extra* time?

2. How would you like to reinvent the work that you do?

Retreat 10:10

How can we navigate ourselves in life?

Realignment

Realignment is a new start.
It is not more of the same.
It is not the continuation
of what we were doing.

Realignment is a fresh start.
It is a complete reframing.
It is the repositioning
of who we are and what we do.

DAILY DEFLECTION – QUESTIONS

1. How well are you navigating your work and career journey?

2. How well are you navigating your life journey?

3. Are they going towards all that really matters for you?

4. Where do you need to realign yourself for a new start?

Retreat 1 – Notes and Key Points

Day 1

_____

_____

_____

Day 2

_____

_____

_____

Day 3

_____

_____

_____

Day 4

_____

_____

_____

Day 5

_____

_____

_____

Day 6

_____

_____

_____

Day 7

_____

_____

_____

Overall thoughts about the week

_____

_____

_____

_____

Points to take with me on the journey

_____

_____

_____

_____

Personal Development Retreat

11

How can we measure gratitude?

Overflow

Today I have a sense
of everything being here and now.
Past, present and future
is all here.

Family and friends long gone
are with me in the garden.
Problems, difficulties and worries
have dissolved in the sunshine.

The blue sky holds
everything below in its care,
and the sun
warms me.

All exists without angst or worry.
Gratitude, excitement, contentment
and a sense of privilege
fill me to overflowing.

DAILY DEFLECTION – QUESTIONS

1. Sit for a moment and hold your past, present and future together – all here now. Let go of anxieties. Who are the family and friends in your story?

2. Feel the warmth of their love and allow your gratitude to overflow.

What's happening beneath the surface?

Iceberg

If we spend all of our time
looking at what's happening,
planning and organising
and sorting out stuff,
we will miss what's happening
beneath the surface
where a whole other world exists,
where 80% of our life is happening.

DAILY DEFLECTION – QUESTIONS

1. What is happening beneath the surface in your life?

2. What are you going to do with all of this hidden potential?

What business are you in?

Market Share

It's not about
keeping the customer satisfied.
It's not about
meeting client needs.
It's not about
responding to gaps in the market.

It's not about
finding your niche.
It's not about
selling more of your stuff.
It's not about
being famous or in demand.

It's not about
the brand or your reputation.
It's not about
anything out there.
It's about
saying what you have to say.

DAILY DEFLECTION – QUESTIONS

1. What are you trying to achieve in your career/business?

2. What are you selling, promoting or marketing?

3. What is it that you have to say?

Who might be struggling at this time?

Remote Control

I met someone today
who is really struggling.
She is carrying so much more
than I could ever imagine.

She spoke so little,
and I have no idea
of what she is trying to
cope with at home.

The success of others around her,
instead of encouraging her,
only seems to magnify
her pain.

I do not know how to respond
to the dullness in her eyes.

Words do not seem to help,
for they only emphasise
the chasm between us,
and where she is stranded.

All I can do is to try
and be there
and to ask love
to sort it out, please.

DAILY DEFLECTION – QUESTIONS

1. Who do you know that is struggling?

2. What can you do to help?

What is a good to-do list?

To-Do List

Today I gave myself nothing to do.
I scrapped my to-do list.
I'm in the park without my phone.
I'm sitting in the sunshine,
enjoying just being here.
Just being.

There are always things to do,
jobs to catch up on,
deadlines and demands from others.
It all has to be done, but not today.
Today I'm sitting, in the sunshine.
Just sitting.

DAILY DEFLECTION – QUESTIONS

1. What's on your to-do list today?

2. When will you be just sitting in the sunshine?

How does your soul talk to you?

Highway Code

The signs are there for you.
Watch out for them.
They're not billboards
and they're not traffic signs.
They are beneath the coincidences
that happen around you.

Signs are moments of feeling,
of awareness and sensitivity,
when windows of light open
and you know that something
is significant or special,
or just meant to be.

Are you open to the signs,
to see and listen to what is here,
and to follow with a thank-you?
For deep down, this is how
your soul talks
and works with you.

DAILY DEFLECTION – QUESTIONS

1. When did you last sense that something was special or just meant to be?

2. How will you respond the next time you get this feeling or awareness?

Are you coming back to the house?

Open Door Policy

There may be storms outside
but inside all is calm.

There may be darkness outside
but inside all is sunny.

There may be fog outside
but inside all is clear.

Forget the weather
and come back to the house.

DAILY DEFLECTION – QUESTIONS

1. What is your weather like today? What are your storms? What is your darkness? What is the fog?

2. Tell me about the house...

How can we live forever?

Timescale

Time is not a linear concept.
It is a circle.
It is the never-ending present,
for there is no start and no finish.

Live in this moment,
for it holds all moments,
and as you live in all moments,
you live forever.

DAILY DEFLECTION – QUESTIONS

1. Draw your life as a complete circle. Where have you placed everything – people, events, relationships, understanding...?

2. What is on the rim of your circle? What sits within the rim? What is at the very centre? What is outside your circle?

Is your purpose the same as your career?

Career Development Strategy

I was building my career and income
and learning to live my purpose through this.

Now I'm delivering on my purpose
and building my career and income through this.

DAILY DEFLECTION – QUESTIONS

1. What is your career development strategy?

2. How can your purpose help to steer your career?

How many steps did you take today?

Steps

Every morning around seven,
two women arrive
outside our house
on their morning walk.

They are chatting
as they walk briskly,
getting in their steps
and sorting out everything in their heads.

Our house is the
turning point on their walk.
They change direction and
head back to their separate days.

We too can create a new routine
for going out and coming back each day,
getting in our steps
and sorting out everything in our heads.

DAILY DEFLECTION – QUESTIONS

1. Who do you talk with when you walk?

2. What or where is your turning point?

Retreat 11 – Notes and Key Points

Day 1

_____

_____

_____

Day 2

_____

_____

_____

Day 3

_____

_____

_____

Day 4

_____

_____

_____

Day 5

_____

_____

_____

Day 6

_____

_____

_____

Day 7

_____

_____

_____

Overall thoughts about the week

_____

_____

_____

_____

Points to take with me on the journey

_____

_____

_____

_____

Personal Development Retreat

12

Is spatial recognition the same as prayer?

Spatial Recognition

There is no set formula
for words in prayer.
Every conversation is different.

For it's not about talking.
It's about sitting patiently
and waiting.

Not for some miraculous
words of wisdom,
but for a gentle thought.

This is prayer.
Sitting, quietly waiting
and leaving space for that thought.

DAILY DEFLECTION – QUESTIONS

1. Where and when will you sit quietly today – leaving space for
   that thought?

2. The process of prayer is bespoke for each of us. I use the phrase
   spatial recognition to describe prayer. What word or phrase
   would you use?

What is your dream?

Collaboration

The sky gives me perspective.
Ideas create my map.
Random thoughts plot coordinates.
Crazy dreams show alternatives.

Harry, the bird, sits on the roof
to help, wherever I go.
Time has stopped for me,
and friends fuel the dream.

DAILY DEFLECTION – QUESTIONS

1. Who or what is collaborating with you?

2. What is the dream?

Is today really your birthday?

Happy Birthday

Imagine that you arrived born
into the world at the age you are now.
Imagine that today was your first day,
your birthday.

You will meet your family,
partner and friends
for the first time.
You will see the house where you live.

You will see trees and water.
You will go to work for the first time,
meet your colleagues
and see how you're using your talents.

Today, on this, your birthday,
you will see all that has been given to you.
You will find out all the roles
where you make your mark.

As you begin to take it all in, you're filled
with wonder, excitement and questions.
You just can't wait to get started,
to find out more and to explore.

It's just so amazing,
what you've been given on this, your birthday.
And then, you receive the most
amazing birthday present of all time.

You will have a new birthday like this,
every single day for the rest of your life.
A new day will arrive,
ready to be discovered.

DAILY DEFLECTION – QUESTIONS

1. Imagine that today is your very first day alive. Where would you start?

2. Where will you explore? How will you capture the wonder and excitement? What questions will you ask?

3. What will you do at the end of this amazing birthday?

Why are those on the ground really in control?

The Seesaw Moment

We can often get caught up
in our moments of progress
or success as our sense of pride
in our achievement floods through.

I love that seesaw moment when
we recognise the person on the ground
who has made this moment happen,
and true balance is restored.

DAILY DEFLECTION – QUESTIONS

1. How do you usually react to moments of progress or success?

2. How do you ensure that you recognise the efforts of those who helped you achieve your success?

3. How do you handle situations when you are the person on the ground?

Do you suffer from impostor syndrome?

Limiting Beliefs

We can see the door
and not open it.

We can approach the gate
and not go through it.

We can be told the path
and not take it.

We can be shown a new way
and not go there.

DAILY DEFLECTION – QUESTIONS

1. What negative thoughts are holding you back from doing all you want to do?

2. All is possible through love – and we are made of love. You can be all you should be. Open the door. Go through the gate. Take the path. Start your new way.

How do you respond to breaking news?

Breaking News

All the birds
are chirping away
loudly and enthusiastically,
all talking at the same time.
It's deafening!

And then, total silence
as they fly off together
to do what they must do,
responding to breaking news
in their world.

DAILY DEFLECTION – QUESTIONS

1. What breaking news would you like to share with the world?

2. How might you do this?

Time is money, or is it?

Clocking in

You cannot buy me.
Simply because I earn money
by the hour or for the job,
doesn't mean that the business has bought me.
For time is only one of my assets.

At work I hold my thinking,
develop my ideas and work out my plans.
So, I do not give all of me
in exchange for money,
just the tasks you want completed.

Time is only one asset that I have.
So, I use my time not just for this job
but to think and reflect on
all parts of my life
and where I plan to be.

DAILY DEFLECTION – QUESTIONS

1. What do you think about at work?

2. How are you balancing the importance of earning a living with pursuing your passions and personal growth?

3. In what ways can you make the most of your time, both professionally and personally?

Is there such a thing as magic?

Magic Show

The most curious thing we can witness
is an impossible magic trick.
Everyone wants to know
the secret!

Yet, for most,
the secret is a disappointment.
The magic is gone
and will never come back.

Sometimes, the magic lies
in the joy
of not knowing
everything.

DAILY DEFLECTION – QUESTIONS

1. What is the one thing, deep down, that you would really love to know?

2. Might it be better to enjoy the magic and not rush to work it out?

Guest post by Tomas McCabe – International Mind Reader and Magician www.tomasmccabe.com

Email Des McCabe with your Guest Post: diversiton@gmail.com

Are you waiting for something to arrive?

One-Day Delivery

True understanding
cannot be accessed by us.
Our normal tools of thinking, reading,
listening and reflecting are of little use.

For this toolkit
can only help us to make sense
of what is already in our heads,
what we already know.

We have to receive new thoughts,
inspiration and ideas from outside
to help us to make sense
of what is going on.

True understanding
is outside of us.
Our toolkit is of little use –
until the package arrives.

DAILY DEFLECTION – QUESTIONS

1. What do you not understand?

2. What package would you like to arrive tomorrow?

Have you written your personal operations manual?

Operations Manual

Today I'm going to be a bit radical.
I'm going to break my rules.
I'm going to do things differently.
I'm not going to follow
my normal routine.

Today will take on a life
and a process and a
perfect purpose of its own.
Whatever happens, happens.
If it feels right, I'll do it.

Today I'm going to trust
in the deeper part of myself,
the one that is so often trapped
or locked away.
Today will see a different me.

I'm rewriting my Operations Manual;
looking at the sky,
walking somewhere different,
just smiling and loving
being with myself.

DAILY DEFLECTION – QUESTIONS

1. Write the Contents page of your personal Operations Manual.

2. Now write the Introduction as if you were talking to yourself.

Retreat 12 – Notes and Key Points

Day 1

_____

_____

_____

Day 2

_____

_____

_____

Day 3

_____

_____

_____

Day 4

_____

_____

_____

Day 5

_____

_____

_____

Day 6

_____

_____

_____

Day 7

_____

_____

_____

Overall thoughts about the week

_____

_____

_____

_____

Points to take with me on the journey

_____

_____

_____

_____

Personal Development Retreat

13

Are we there yet?

_____

Eternal Now

This is a spiritual journey,
not a business or work one.
This is the journey in my eternal now,
not a plan for the next year.

This is a journey beyond this place,
not a marketing or income strategy.
This is a journey away from me,
not a reliance on myself.

This is a journey that cannot be described,
not one plotted by success or failure.
This is a journey without family or friends,
and without myself.

DAILY DEFLECTION – QUESTIONS

1. What is your spiritual journey?

2. How can you recognise this journey in your daily life?

3. What does the concept of the *eternal now* mean to you?

How should we start each day?

Alarm Call

Started in work mode.
Straight onto my phone.
Planning the day.
Checking my appointments.
Writing my to-do list.
Forgot to smile
and say good morning
to the one I love.

DAILY DEFLECTION – QUESTIONS

1. What is the first thing you do each morning when you awaken?

2. How can you create a more mindful mindset in the mornings?

3. What new habits might you develop to reflect your priorities and values?

4. Where is your smile?

What will you say to yourself today?

Daily Blog

Start your daily blog today.
Grab a notebook.
Put *Day One* on the first page
and write something.

This is a blog for you,
not for the world;
not for marketing your products
or promoting your expertise.

This is your daily feedback,
conversation and notes for yourself.
It's your life training manual
to underpin all that you do.

These are the words that tell you
what's really happening around you
and within you.
It's only for you.

And as you build your blog
day by day,
you will see themes develop,
ideas flourish and a plan emerge.

You will build a greater sense
of who you really are.
Every day, write your blog.
Grab a notebook – start today.

It is here where seeds
can be planted and can flourish.
For if you write it down,
it can become real.

Capture what's happening
or isn't happening.
Capture all the joy and gratitude
and all that causes you pain.

For your daily blog
is an ongoing conversation
with all that really matters.
Start your daily blog today.

DAILY DEFLECTION – QUESTIONS

1. What would you like to say to yourself today?

2. And how will yourself respond?

Is community cohesion the same as inclusion?

Community Cohesion

A new community will emerge.
A new type of community
will emerge and grow,
offering help and hope.

A new definition of community
will emerge and grow,
changing the *why* and the *how*
and serving all.

For community is not an organisation
or a structure.
Community is not based in a place,
or even in a virtual space.

Community rests in each of us,
enabling us
to reach outwards
and to work with all others.

DAILY DEFLECTION – QUESTIONS

1. How can you build a new type of personal community?

2. What will you work on?

3. Who will you offer help and hope to?

Is today a holy day?

Holy Days

There were no visits to a church.
There was no kneeling in prayer.
There were no readings.
There was no sitting in silence

and yet

today was the holiest of days.
I spent every moment with you
working tirelessly
on the project.

DAILY DEFLECTION – QUESTIONS

1. What is your project?

2. How is today a holy day for you?

What is personal leadership?

Tow Rope

The world keeps
pulling us back
to its way of working,
to follow its rules,
to behave in the way
that it wants us to be.

Untie the rope.

The world keeps
taking us to places
away from where we want to be,
away from all we value,
away from our true selves,
to be dependent on it.

Untie your rope.

DAILY DEFLECTION – QUESTIONS

1. How is the world pulling you back?

2. How is the world taking you away from where you should be?

3. How can you untie your rope?

Daily Deflections

Retreat 13.7

What is a personal staycation?

Staycation

Go beyond the junk
always.
See past the hassle
always.
And stay where you are.

Look at the bigger picture
always.
Be true to yourself
always.
And stay where you are.

Get rid of the distractions
always.
Discard what is unnecessary
always.
And stay where you are.

DAILY DEFLECTION – QUESTIONS

1. What can you do to go beyond the junk and be true to yourself?

2. Where are you staying?

252

What is life by numbers?

Colouring by Numbers

When I was a child, I had a book called
Colouring by Numbers.
The outlines of everything
were all there in the picture.
I just had to colour in the spaces.

Areas with One were blue
and those with Two were yellow
and so on.
The picture came alive in front of me.
The outcome was complete and perfect!

Imagine that you could have the outline of your life
as a picture, ready to be filled in now.
It would mean that we wouldn't live
on the basis of process or journey,
thinking about what happens next year,
or what our next job will be.

It'll all be there in the outline.
We just need to follow the numbers
in any order we want.
Nothing will be left out.
All will be complete and perfect.
Draw your outline!

DAILY DEFLECTION – QUESTIONS

1. What would you include in your picture?

2. Is it about events, people, success, happiness?

3. Who else is in the picture, and what's in the background?

Do we lose our creativity with artificial intelligence?

Artificial Intelligence

Years ago, when we were travelling
we would stop at a lay-by,
take out our map
and plan our route.

We would create options,
factor in a coffee break
at a little village,
and plot a route that worked for us.

Now we put our destination
into our phone, which is more efficient.
The route is planned for us
and we do not have to think.

We don't pause in the lay-by.
We don't create our options.
We don't stop in the little village.
We just go where we're told.

DAILY DEFLECTION – QUESTIONS

1. What options and opportunities are you creating?

2. Where is your little village?

Are time and activity driving who you are?

Headmaster

I am still in the office at home.
I am still at work.
My head is full of stuff.
The number of things to do
seems to be getting longer, not shorter.

For as soon as I cross something off the list,
another two things appear, needing to be done.
My brain and my whole self are consumed
and controlled by this list
of what needs to be done.

I can't just walk away from it
for it all needs to be sorted.
And who else will do it if I don't?
If this day was twice as long, I would fill it.
If it was shorter, I would cram even more in.

Then it hits me that I am being managed
by the time available – not by who I am.
I have it all the wrong way round.
For it's not about doing, but being.
Being is the master of time, my Headmaster.

DAILY DEFLECTION – QUESTIONS

1. What is your Headmaster?

2. How do time and activity drive who you are?

3. What does *being* mean to you – in practical terms?

Retreat 13 – Notes and Key Points

Day 1

_____

_____

_____

Day 2

_____

_____

_____

Day 3

_____

_____

_____

Day 4

_____

_____

_____

Day 5

_____

_____

_____

Day 6

_____

_____

_____

Day 7

_____

_____

_____

Overall thoughts about the week

_____

_____

_____

_____

Points to take with me on the journey

_____

_____

_____

_____

Personal Development Retreat

14

What have you received this week?

Delivery Confirmation

It's time to write
this week's list of thank-yous.
Where will you start?
Where was your joy?

What have you learned?
What have you been given?
What was the one big surprise?
Who has helped you?

What has been sorted?
How have you been?
Who did you speak with?
What did you take for granted?

It's Saturday and it's time
to write this week's list of thank-yous,
to sign here for all
that you have received.

DAILY DEFLECTION – QUESTIONS

1. What have been the key events and memories of the last seven days?

2. Write down your top 10 thank-yous – and then rank them in order of importance for you, from 1 to 10.

What is inward marketing?

Inward Marketing

True marketing is an inward
rather than an outward process.
Outward marketing means
that we can spend our lives
chasing customers,
coming up with the latest product or service
and repeating this again and again,
just like we are told we need to do.

Inward marketing means
that we are personally driven.
We look inwards to our core skills,
beliefs, gifts, passions and interests.
We work out who and what we are.
And then we have exactly
what the world is missing
and urgently needs.

DAILY DEFLECTION - QUESTIONS

1. Make a list of your core skills, experience, interests and passions.

2. Now add your values and beliefs (what's important to you) to help work out who and what you are.

3. How might you share all of this with the world?

What is inactive leadership?

Action Leadership

We see a lack of activity
as being ineffective
or a waste of resources
or being lazy
or not productive.

We have forgotten
how to sit and wait,
to be content
and trust that all is well.

DAILY DEFLECTION – QUESTIONS

1. Do you take time to be ineffective, lazy, and non-productive?

2. Have you learned to sit and trust that all is well?

3. Do you know what you are waiting for?

What is the liquid of life?

Liquidity

We become so busy in life
doing all we should
and getting on with everything,
that it is easy to forget to look closely
and assess it all.

This is more than
thinking about where we are
or planning our future.
It's about something internal
beyond all our actions.

It's about going closer
towards the essence of life itself,
being part of the liquid of life
flowing through all of us
as one.

DAILY DEFLECTION – QUESTIONS

1. What is the liquid of life that connects and flows through all of us?

2. How can you boost and improve that liquidity – to benefit yourself and all others?

Can we recycle all that we are?

Recycling

The priority each day
is to reposition yourself
closer to the source.

Rethink all that you are,
recreate all that you do
and refocus on what you are to become.

DAILY DEFLECTION – QUESTIONS

1. Every day is a fresh start. Our old self is recycled to be made new again. What are you going to be today?

2. And how will you recreate yourself tomorrow?

Where can we find happiness?

Home Security

I sat patiently
on the beach,
not moving.
I sat there for hours.

And then I felt
a different sensation
as the tide
slowly came in.

No waves, no noise.
Quietly and gently,
the sea lifted me
off the stones.

I swayed left and right,
forwards and backwards,
for what seemed like a lifetime,
not knowing what to do.

And still the tide came in.
It started to move me outwards,
leading me further
from my place of safety.

I drifted away
on an uncharted journey,
happy and content
to find a new beach in time.

DAILY DEFLECTION – QUESTIONS

1. Can you trust in the process and let go of your place of safety?

2. How will you journey and find your new beach?

Can we outsource our life?

Outsourcing

Don't do everything yourself.
Share your dream with the world.
Collaborate with others.
Reach out and build your team.
For when we don't try to do everything,
we can do anything.

Don't do everything yourself.
Create projects and initiatives.
Let others work with you.
Set out the plan and make it happen.
For when we let it all go,
we will all do everything.

DAILY DEFLECTION – QUESTIONS

1. How will you work with others so that they can help and support you?

2. Who is (and will be) on your team?

3. We all have a dream to share with the world. What's yours?

When should we start again?

Starter

We mess up.
We learn.
We start again.

We got it wrong.
We think about it.
We start again.

We let others down.
We are disappointed.
We start again.

We failed to deliver.
We are annoyed.
We start again.

We got caught out.
We are embarrassed.
We start again.

We missed the opportunity.
We are frustrated.
We start again.

We see it fall apart.
We are devastated.
We start again.

DAILY DEFLECTION – QUESTIONS

1. Is there anything that you need to forgive yourself for? You can start again.

2. Is there anything that you need to forgive others for? You can start again. It's never too late. Be the starter!

Will you become a first responder today?

First Responder

When tragedy strikes around the world
we see images of destruction and death.
There's pain and anguish on young faces.

It's easy to feel helpless.
But there are six key things we can do
in these moments.

We can be with the families,
not just as onlookers, but in our thoughts.
We can feel and share some of their pain.

We can send our message of love right now,
personal and direct. We can offer ourselves
and all that we are to support them.

We can give money through agencies.
And we can encourage our friends to do likewise.
Our one small gift can begin an avalanche.

We can create and say a prayer of love.
It's our call to the power of God to rescue,
change, heal and renew.

We can commit to specific actions
to help create a kinder and more caring world
as we move forward in our own lives.

And we can encourage our children, young people
and colleagues to become First Responders
when they too hear the news.

Those struggling are not in some far-off land
or on our screens, separate from us.
They are beside us, now.

DAILY DEFLECTION – QUESTIONS

1. What is the role of a First Responder?

2. Think about the latest world tragedy and see how many of the six points you can do.

3. Imagine that we were the ones who were suffering, and it was our tragedy on the news.

What are the three main types of thinking?

Thinking Skills

If we wake up
and then just pick up
where we left off yesterday,
we are doing more
of what we have already done.
This is cumulative thinking.

If we wake up
and then something unexpected hits us,
we are lost and rudderless,
our world is turned inside out
and we are unsure what to do next.
This is reactive thinking.

If we wake up
and then choose to pick up
something new or different today,
we are creating a fresh challenge.
We are uncovering our new way.
This is deliberate thinking.

DAILY DEFLECTION – QUESTIONS

1. What thought can help you to uncover your new way today?

2. Can you identify those times when you might be more prone to cumulative and reactive thinking?

3. What changes might you need to make to get closer to deliberate thinking?

Retreat 14 – Notes and Key Points

Day 1

_____

_____

_____

Day 2

_____

_____

_____

Day 3

_____

_____

_____

Day 4

_____

_____

_____

Day 5

_____

_____

_____

Day 6

_____

_____

_____

Day 7

_____

_____

_____

Overall thoughts about the week

_____

_____

_____

_____

Points to take with me on the journey

_____

_____

_____

_____

Personal Development Retreat

15

What does it mean to be *in the zone*?

In the Zone

'You have to be in the zone,' she said.
'You have to focus your mind,
be in a different place
and bring all to bear
on the task.'

And then she smiled and said,
'And from here, you can find the real zone,
which is beyond all tasks
and beyond all thinking,
where no zone can be.'

DAILY DEFLECTION – QUESTIONS

1. What does being in the zone mean to you, and how can you cultivate a state of focus and flow in your life?

2. How might you strike a better balance between the need to get things done and cultivating space for stillness and reflection?

3. What are some techniques or habits that you might incorporate into your daily routine?

What is the purpose of reincarnation?

Reincarnation

No one ever dies.
No kindness is ever wasted.
No one is ever lost.
For everything just changes
into love.

DAILY DEFLECTION – QUESTIONS

1. How are you growing gently into love?

2. Looking back, what have been the key phases or times in your life (so far) where you have seen or felt the impact of love?

What does your ideal job look like?

Online Job Application

What is your current job?
Please don't use your job title.

Who do you work for?
Please don't put your business name
or your boss's name here!

What do you work for?
Please go beyond money.

What do you actually do?
Please go beyond your job description.

What does your ideal job look like?
Please say what you'd really like to do.

My job is to help others
to understand their lives better.
I work for a *kinder* world.
I work for *love*.
I encourage people to be
all that they can be.

DAILY DEFLECTION – QUESTIONS

1. Put all five answers together.

2. Send this to yourself and ask, 'What does it say to me?'

Have you a fear of dying?

Appointment Reminder

In the middle of the night,
when all is so dark and empty,
there is nothing for me to see or do.
My mind shoots me back to that
dreaded place I knew well when I was 17,
fearing death and my non-existence.

These momentary incisions literally
shake me as I am overwhelmed
by some uncontrollable force.
The panic attack, as they named it,
has returned tonight.
It's terrifying.

It was somehow different back then
as I had my whole life before me.
I could rationalise it and it would pass.
Now it's not so straightforward.
But as I've got older, I've seen that this dread
is, in fact, a blessing of love.

I've learned that the losing of my self
is what we all ultimately
move through in dying.
We each have to let go
of what we are so desperate not to lose
as we become everything that is love.

It is no surprise to me tonight
that my brain still struggles
and refuses to let go.
For it knows now that this is simply
another reminder,
and not the appointment.

DAILY DEFLECTION – QUESTIONS

1. How do you cope with feelings of fear or panic related to death?

2. How has your perspective on dying changed as you have grown older?

3. How might losing your self allow you to become everything that is love?

What is the sharing economy?

Sharing Economy

I sit on Platform 2
on a lovely mild and sunny August day
with a cup of tea
and some crunchy oat and honey biscuits.
Three pigeons keep me company,
making sure that we leave nothing behind.

DAILY DEFLECTION – QUESTIONS

1. How can you help others on your journey?

2. Who is in your sharing economy?

When do you stop for a cold beer?

Call to Prayer

The church clock in our little village
chimes at 3 o'clock as I cut the grass.
It's my call to prayer,
and I pause for a moment.

At 4 o'clock we repeat the process.
It seems like a fitting end point,
working to God's time.
Time for thanks and a cold beer.

DAILY DEFLECTION – QUESTIONS

1. When do you pause in your day to give thanks?

2. What small rituals do you weave into your day?

What's the alternative to the rat race?

Rat Race

We have inherited a world
where jobs and work
are allocated to people.

Employers work out the tasks
that need to be done,
and carve up the activity.

It's an outdated economic model
where we are paid to do what we are told.
And many have no jobs.

With technology we can now
create work in different ways,
driven by what really matters.

We can link up with others
and collaborate on projects
that are important to us as individuals.

We can take responsibility
for creating and shaping all of our futures
and a better world.

We can share resources
rather than wait, like rats,
for the food pellets to arrive.

DAILY DEFLECTION – QUESTIONS

1. How can you use your skills, experience and passions in new ways?

2. Who can you start to work with today to create your new projects?

What picture are you creating today?

Weather Forecast

I look at the early morning sky.
It is a blank canvas.

By lunchtime I will have filled in
half of this picture.

By tonight it will all be complete.
And what will this picture be?

Whether or not it will be the picture I planned
remains to be seen.

DAILY DEFLECTION – QUESTIONS

1. Look up at the sky where you are – go on, do this now!

2. This sky is your blank canvas for the rest of this day. What picture are you planning to paint?

How do you manage your energy supply?

Energy Supply

Some days I wake up
full of energy,
ready to get moving
and excited about the day ahead.

Some days I wake up
lacklustre, weary,
struggling to get going
to face the tasks ahead.

Today is an energy day,
just like yesterday!
I must be on a roll.
It's so good to be alive.

I must capitalise on this potential.
I have to get it all done.
For tomorrow, who knows?
I could be in low power mode.

These are not good days or bad days
for every day is a good day.
It's simply me
managing my energy supply.

DAILY DEFLECTION – QUESTIONS

1. What is your energy level like today? Are you ready to go for it?

2. What is your plan for low energy days? Remember, all days have something special to teach us – so how can you accept slower days with joy?

Is it time to think about your next holiday?

Holiday

My mind is busy running over
all of the current activities.
It's as if I'm living in them,
rather than just completing them
and moving on.

I seem to want to hold it all
in my head,
and replay the elements over and over again –
where I did well
or where I messed up.

I shift down a gear
and leave all the daily activity to one side.
Travelling slower, I can plan and organise.
There is more space for thinking here.
It is quieter.

And then I go even slower
and bring the car to a halt,
leaving all thinking behind.
Sitting quietly by the shore
and looking out to sea.

DAILY DEFLECTION – QUESTIONS

1. Are you holding anything in your head to replay over and over again?

2. When is your next holiday moment – when you can sit quietly and look out to sea...?

Retreat 15 – Notes and Key Points

Day 1

_____

_____

_____

Day 2

_____

_____

_____

Day 3

_____

_____

_____

Day 4

_____

_____

_____

Day 5

_____

_____

_____

Day 6

_____

_____

_____

Day 7

_____

_____

_____

Overall thoughts about the week

_____

_____

_____

_____

Points to take with me on the journey

_____

_____

_____

_____

Personal Development Retreat

16

What are the top 10 Thank-Yous?

Short-Term Memory

We awaken each day.
We go to sleep.
We forget to say thanks.

We eat our food.
We wear our clothes.
We forget to say thanks.

We have our home.
We have our world.
We forget to say thanks.

We walk and talk.
We laugh and cry.
We forget to say thanks.

We have our family.
We have our friends.
We forget to say thanks.

We have our work.
We have our rest.
We forget to say thanks.

We have time to be busy.
We have time to rest.
We forget to say thanks.

We can think and dream.
We can plan and prepare.
We forget to say thanks.

We can be happy or sad.
We can be ourselves.
We forget to say thanks.

We were born and given life.
We have wonderful memories.
We forget to say thanks.

Everything has been given to us
for all that we are.
We stop and give thanks.

DAILY DEFLECTION – QUESTIONS

1. Just stop for a moment and give thanks for all that you are.

2. Write down your top ten Thank-Yous, and remember to say them every day.

How can we hold each other?

Holding Company

It is the pot that holds the soup.
It is our soup.
It is the universe that holds the world.
It is our world.
It is the arm that holds the child.
It is our child.
It is the book that holds the word.
It is our word.
It is the face that holds a smile.
It is our smile.
It is the light that holds our life.
It is our life.

DAILY DEFLECTION – QUESTIONS

1. Who or what do you hold in your life?

2. Who or what holds you?

What do we look for in the mirror?

Reflection

We can only really
see ourselves properly
when we look in a mirror.
The reflection comes
straight back to us.
Our bathroom mirror
shows us how we look today.

We can only really
know ourselves fully
when we look to see God.
The reflection comes
straight back and shows us,
just like a mirror,
all that we really are.

Until we look,
there can be no reflection.
There is no picture.
There is no image.
Until we look to see God,
there can be no real
understanding of self.

DAILY DEFLECTION – QUESTIONS

1. What do you see when you look in your bathroom mirror?

2. Where else can you look to know yourself better?

What is food for thought?

Servant Leadership

We wait at
the table
for our food.

We wait
on the table
and bring the food.

DAILY DEFLECTION – QUESTIONS

1. In what ways can the principles of servant leadership be incorporated into our work roles?

2. How can applying servant leadership to those we care for strengthen our relationship?

3. How might adopting a mindset of servant leadership benefit you?

Is life one long sentence?

Life Sentence

In this moment,
a thought is born
and the idea comes.
The words flow
and the writing
takes shape,
ready to share.

Every moment
holds a thought,
so let your ideas come,
your words flow
and your writing
take shape.
You're ready to share.

DAILY DEFLECTION – QUESTIONS

1. Create a moment each day just to catch your thoughts...

2. Remember: our thoughts are unique, and they are our treasure. How can we share them?

What is the word?

Word

Thinking differently about everything
encourages us to focus on a word,
and to hold this word.

We place this word at the centre
of our hearts and allow it
to grow in these moments.

It is in this process that we move
beyond our normal definitions
of words and meanings.

We try not to get distracted,
and keep coming back to this word
resting gently within us.

It is only when we free the word
to be, in and of itself,
that it becomes all that it should be.

We then become one with the word
within us, for we are the word
and the word is with God.

DAILY DEFLECTION – QUESTIONS

1. Choose a word, sit quietly for ten minutes, and just hold this word gently within you.

2. Images and feeling will emerge after a short time. Follow these. Then write it all down.

What is our message for the world?

Communication Skills

Uncover your message.
Write your words.
Capture your stories.

Keep a journal.
Update it each day.
Include your case studies.

Harvest all that you are.
For the world needs
your grace and your love.

Start a blog.
Post your updates.
Publish your books.

Create your courses.
Record your podcasts.
Make your videos.

Share all that you are.
For the world needs
your grace and your love.

DAILY DEFLECTION – QUESTIONS

1. What have you seen and learned over the years?
2. What are your messages for the world?

How can we make the impossible possible?

Instant Access

To get from here to there
is just impossible.
I know from experience
that it just can't be done.

Scientifically, it is not possible
and I have no idea
where to even start.
There is no map.

It has never been done before.
So, my brain can only
see the outcome
and not the steps.

But if I can
see the outcome,
then I have already left where I was.
I am here.

DAILY DEFLECTION – QUESTIONS

1. What is your impossible destination?

2. Don't worry about the journey. Can you focus on actually being there – right now?

Retreat 16.9

What do we put in the suitcase of the future?

Suitcase

So much of our focus and time today
will be about the here and now.

Much of our focus will be on ourselves
and what we need to do,
or what we have to achieve.

We have the wrong perspective though,
for our focus and time today
should be on what comes next.

Our focus should be about
what we have to sort out
and do to get ready.

We need to work out
what we are putting in our suitcase.

DAILY DEFLECTION – QUESTIONS

1. Where are you going?

2. What are you putting in your suitcase?

Where is your haven of peace?

Venture Capital

The taxi collects me at 8:40am
from my work hotel in Bahrain
and takes me some 20 minutes
to the Sacred Heart Church in Manama.

The driver and I
have enough English between us
to arrange for him
to come back for me at 11am.

I spend two hours
captive in this compound
with no distractions.
It's a haven of peace for me.

I leave at 10:58am
and my driver is here,
waiting to take me back
to my hotel and swimming pool.

314

DAILY DEFLECTION – QUESTIONS

1. Where is your haven of peace?

2. What do you do on a morning you are not working?

3. What is your next new venture?

Retreat 16 – Notes and Key Points

Day 1

_____

_____

_____

Day 2

_____

_____

_____

Day 3

_____

_____

_____

Day 4

_____

_____

_____

Day 5

_____

_____

_____

Day 6

_____

_____

_____

Day 7

_____

_____

_____

Overall thoughts about the week

_____

_____

_____

_____

Points to take with me on the journey

_____

_____

_____

_____

Personal Development Retreat

17

What is your positioning statement?

Positioning Statement

I had a mentoring call
with an author in New York yesterday
from my rural base in the UK.

'How are you today?' she asked.
'I'm brilliant!' I responded.
She looked at me quizzically.

After a pause, she said, 'Here in the US,
that means you're like Einstein,
a genius, incredibly clever?'

I laughed.
'No, I just meant I am in really good form.'
And we arrived on the same page.

I learned about her work,
empowering those who felt inadequate,
and the millions of people she had helped.

At the end of the call, she said 'Thanks!'
I smiled and said, 'You are brilliant!'
And we laughed.

How are you today?

DAILY DEFLECTION – QUESTIONS

1. What do you say when others ask, 'How are you today?'
2. How often do you tell others that they are brilliant?

Are we all still on induction training?

Induction Training

Whatever age you are,
it doesn't really matter.
The reality is that
you haven't even started yet.

Don't let memory or routine
or disappointment hold you back.
Get ready now,
for you haven't even started yet.

There are no expectations.
The world is there for you.
It is yours to embrace.
You haven't even started yet.

Your life is in front of you.
All potential
and possibilities are here.
You haven't even started yet.

For this is the moment
beyond all moments,
when you finally realise that
you haven't even started yet.

DAILY DEFLECTION – QUESTIONS

1. Everything up to now has been a preparation for what is to come. Everything starts from today. What are you going to do?

2. What might be holding you back?

How can we repurpose our lives?

Repurpose

Perhaps it is time
to clear out the attic?

Perhaps all that has been
gathered up over the years
needs to be thrown away
or used in a different way?

Perhaps we need to get back
to the house of years ago?
Free of clutter, freshly painted
and full of possibilities.

DAILY DEFLECTION – QUESTIONS

1. What is in your attic?

2. How can you discover the possibilities that will help you fulfil
   your purpose?

How do I set my hourly rate?

Hourly Rate

Don't just work for money.
Work for the asset
you can create from that time.
Think of the conversation, the experience,
the new knowledge, the case study
and the learning you have just received.

What can you pull out –
or harvest – from this time at work?
What have you learned? Who have you met?
What were the points of interest?
What is new or different
that you can share with others?

We work to be better equipped
to advise, train or help others.
We work to develop and build
upon our expertise or key message.
We work to collect new information
for our next book, service or product.

So, don't sell your time just for money.
Explore the potential in every situation
at work and play, and harvest from this.
After your work has finished, write down
all that you have been given,
for this is where the real value is.

Your hourly rate
is measured not just in money.
Your hourly rate is measured by
all that your work contains, how much
you harvest and then what you share.
This is the gift you must not leave unused.

DAILY DEFLECTION – QUESTIONS

1. What have you harvested from your work today / yesterday / last week?

2. What steps can you take to ensure that you are harvesting as much value as possible from your work experiences?

3. How can you use your work to develop and build upon your expertise and your key message?

4. How will you share all that you are harvesting each day?

Is God part of inclusion?

Religious Belief

Talking about God
is not easy in our world.
It is a conversation
that gets closed down quickly.

It singles us out
and we get placed in a camp.
It's them and me.
It becomes about exclusion.

But their view of God and mine
are worlds apart.
They talk of religion or belief.
I talk of love.

DAILY DEFLECTION – QUESTIONS

1. What does the word *love* mean to you?

2. What does the word *religion* mean to you?

What does success mean to you?

Success

It may not work.
It may not happen.
It may not unfold as we think
or had hoped for.

But this is not failure.
Failure is when we don't have the dream,
when we don't act or
when we don't try to make it happen.

Success is when we do our best,
do what we can
and recognise that this is
what is intended.

DAILY DEFLECTION – QUESTIONS

1. What is your dream?

2. How will you try to make this real today?

What is your hidden agenda?

Hidden Agenda

There are things we should do
but we don't do them.
There are people we should see
but we don't see them.
There is work we should do
but we don't do it.
There are words we should say
but we don't say them.
There are places we should go
but we don't go there.

DAILY DEFLECTION – QUESTIONS

1. What is your hidden agenda – the people and activities that you are avoiding?

2. How can you begin to address this?

Why is it not enough to think outside the box?

Container Business

The original business model was straightforward. It was about profit and building a business. The mill owners of the Industrial Revolution had a simple focus.

Over the years, other elements have impacted upon that business model – employee rights, consumer protection, international laws, staff development, government interventions of all sorts, corporate social responsibility, exchange rates, outsourcing, internet marketing, health and safety and more.

The local business entity of the Industrial Revolution has now become much more complex in a globally interconnected world.

Interestingly though, our concept of what business is and how it should work is still defined by that original model. In short, we keep adding on more hi-tech features to the vehicle without really looking at the 250-year-old chassis. This cumulative approach needs disassembling.

Henry Ford used to make all his cars in black, but those days have long gone. Likewise, the 'one size fits all' approach to business is no longer relevant. Perhaps we should be exploring many models driven not by history but by needs, situations and opportunities – however defined.

Sociology, philosophy, spirituality, psychology, environmentalism, technology and the arts can all offer key insights to new ways in. It's time not just to think outside of the box, but to get out of the box and build new containers.

DAILY DEFLECTION – QUESTIONS

1. Business is now personal. What business are you in?

2. How do you define your model of business – making money and looking after all that you care about?

Why should I become a landscape architect?

Landscape Architect

I am always looking ahead,
thinking, *What next?*
Today's plan? Next week's activities?
Trying to schedule everything in.

But what I don't do
is look at the year ahead,
think about the next three years,
or indeed the next ten years.

I need to lift my thinking
to be more strategic
and not just task-focused.
For life isn't just about weeding.

The future is there to be imagined
and then created.
Seeds need to be planted
for the flowers I want to grow.

DAILY DEFLECTION – QUESTIONS

1. What's your personal strategy for the next year, the next three years, and the next ten years?

2. Write each of these down.

Have you tried cheese mints?

Achievements

My voice recognition software
thinks I'm talking about
cheese mints.

It looks like I've just
created a new product
by accident!

Imagine if this turned out to be
one of my greatest
achievements.

DAILY DEFLECTION – QUESTIONS

1. What has happened recently that has caused you to smile and see things a bit differently?

2. What new product or service would you like to create or offer?

Retreat 17 – Notes and Key Points

Day 1

_____

_____

_____

Day 2

_____

_____

_____

Day 3

_____

_____

_____

Day 4

_____

_____

_____

Day 5

_____

_____

_____

Day 6

_____

_____

_____

Day 7

_____

_____

_____

Overall thoughts about the week

_____

_____

_____

_____

Points to take with me on the journey

_____

_____

_____

_____

Personal Development Retreat

18

Can we create the best gift shop in the world?

Gift Shop

There is no lock.
The door of the gift shop
is always open.

We are invited in
and we are able
to take what we wish.

This is fantastic!
Free gifts galore.
Let's take more of these.

And then we realise that
if we continue,
soon the shop will be empty.

So we stop taking.
Instead, we begin to bring
and to share our own gifts.

For we see now
that together, we can create
the best gift shop in the world.

DAILY DEFLECTION – QUESTIONS

1. What gift can you bring to the best gift shop in the world?

2. What do you enjoy most about the gift shop?

How are your eight friends today?

House Party

My mind is buzzing.
My brain is creating.

My ego is expanding.
My conscience is questioning.

My heart is beating.
My soul is too quiet.

My self is in doubt.
My body is restless.

There's a lot going on
in the house today.

DAILY DEFLECTION – QUESTIONS

1. What's happening in your house today?

2. How are your eight friends – your mind, brain, ego, conscience, heart, soul, self and body?

Does love have a short-term memory?

Short-Term Memory

Love forgives us
for everything,
unconditionally,
no matter what.
Right from now.

Love then forgets
everything that it forgives.
We can start again, afresh,
no matter what.
Right from now.

Love insists that you too
forgive yourself and forget all
that you carry as a burden,
no matter what.
Right from now.

DAILY DEFLECTION – QUESTIONS

1. What do you still need to forgive yourself for? Do it now.

2. There is no longer any burden to carry. Are you ready to start afresh, right from now?

Do we live outwards and inwards?

Parallel Interface

We all live parallel lives.
Our daily work routine, our relationships
and the things that we do
are all part of our outer living.

What goes on in the deep recesses
of our consciousness through our self-reflection
is our inner living.
Both exist together.

DAILY DEFLECTION – QUESTIONS

1. How much time and thought do you give to your inner living?

2. Have you explored how your outer and inner living work seamlessly together?

3. How can you use your outer living experiences to enhance and deepen your inner living – and vice versa?

What message are we copying and pasting everywhere?

Copy and Paste

I typed the word *love*
and saw it
in front of me.

I highlighted the word *love*
and captured it
in my heart.

I copied the word *love*
and made it
who I am.

I pasted the word *love*
and it
was everywhere.

DAILY DEFLECTION – QUESTIONS

1. We copy and paste who we are in every encounter with others. Where can you paste *love* today?

2. What are the other words that are you pasting everywhere? What is the message that others are picking up from us?

343

What is our personal stamp?

Stamp Collection

The world demands
outputs and results,
achievements and success.
But we long for
love and peace,
happiness and health.

We can be dominated
by external events,
or we can choose
to work together,
and create
a different way.

We can be continually
stamped on in an
uncaring and demanding world.
Or we can come together
and gently put our stamp
on all before us.

DAILY DEFLECTION – QUESTIONS

1. How has the world stamped on you in the past?

2. How are you gently putting your stamp on all before you?

Are you needs-driven?

Needs-driven

Embrace all possibilities.
Be open to the unseen potential
in every situation
and in every moment.

Go out.
Just go there, just be there.
And bring with you
all that you are.

Be positive.
Be encouraging.
Be ambitious for your success
and the success of others.

Be gracious.
Be grateful.
Be kind
and smile.

Do what you love.
Enjoy your interests.
Set the world on fire
and watch the grass grow.

And when you realise
that there is nothing
that you really need,
then you have everything.

DAILY DEFLECTION – QUESTIONS

1. How will you set the world on fire and watch the grass grow today?

2. What do you still really need?

What is your business model?

Multi-Level Marketing

I met Fred for the first time today.
He was passionate about trying to
encourage me to join his multi-level
marketing scheme in crypto currencies.
I was puzzled because Fred clearly had
more money than he needed. He'd been
successful in many other ventures.
And he was well into his 70s.

I marvelled at Fred's sense of drive,
his relentless passion and his total
focus on building his team.
'What drives you?' I asked.
He said that when he was younger
he was told that he needed
to have seven streams of income.
He only had six. And he laughed.

How could somebody be totally focused
on building wealth? He was travelling the
country attending meeting after meeting,
promoting all the time and in every
single conversation. He was a true MLM
specialist, living and working with everyone
in his downline. 'But surely life must be
about more than money?' I asked.

Fred smiled and continued, 'My aim
is to generate opportunities
for people, to help them to fulfil
their plans and their destiny.
I also spend my money in ways that
others don't know about. You see,
each of us must find our own way
and then give our all to that.'

DAILY DEFLECTION – QUESTIONS

1. What is your business?

2. Have you found your own way?

3. How does your work help to deliver all that is important for
   you?

What do focus groups tell us?

Focus Group

'I got a sad meal at McDonald's yesterday.'
'Don't you mean a Happy Meal?'
'No, the toy was missing
and I was a little bit sad.'

(two young friends discussing their lunch)

DAILY DEFLECTION – QUESTIONS

1. What would others say, in private, about the product or service that you provide?

2. Are you doing all that you could to make you happy?

Retreat 18.10

What is the takeaway of this moment?

Takeaway

Let us talk of
inward reflection
rather than prayer.

For it is by going inwards
away from the clamour
of the world...

...into the gentle silence,
that we see our real selves
reflected in love.

And this is what
we take into our lives
and all we do.

DAILY DEFLECTION – QUESTIONS

1. Where do you find the gentle silence?

2. When will you have your next takeaway?

Retreat 18 – Notes and Key Points

Day 1

_____

_____

_____

Day 2

_____

_____

_____

Day 3

_____

_____

_____

Day 4

_____

_____

_____

Day 5

_____

_____

_____

Day 6

_____

_____

_____

Day 7

_____

_____

_____

Overall thoughts about the week

_____

_____

_____

_____

Points to take with me on the journey

_____

_____

_____

_____

Personal Development Retreat

19

What is your full menu of possibility?

Beyond the Usual Choices

We get on with our life,
day after day.
We adapt, as circumstances
around us change.

But imagine that
we started afresh without
the expectation of continuing
what we are doing.

What would be
the menu of possibilities
that we could lay out
in front of us?

Of course, we will be
tempted to reject many
of these before they
even get written down.

But capture
all of your options.
Be creative. Be wacky.
Be ambitious.

For it is only when we see
the whole menu
that we can choose
our main course.

DAILY DEFLECTION – QUESTIONS

1. How often do we pause to consider the full range of possibilities in front of us before making decisions?

2. What are some of the limiting beliefs or assumptions that prevent us from seeing a broader menu of options?

3. How can we cultivate a mindset of openness and creativity to generate new possibilities?

How can I create the perfect job description?

Job Description

Our spiritual journey isn't
necessarily a holy or religious one!
We are all called to be part of *love*
in our own unique and special way.

For some, this is in business,
others in acting, others in nursing,
others in sport or teaching,
retail or manufacturing.

But these are only careers or jobs
that describe what we do,
and not who we are. It's who we are
that is the real spiritual journey.

It's how we interact with people.
It's how we reach out.
It's how we help others.
It's the times when we are kind.

This is the real day-to-day spiritual journey
that we are all on.
And it doesn't matter what
our role or job or situation is.

For every connection with others
touches something deep within us.
It gives meaning
to who we are in that moment.

Each interaction connects us
to the same love
that is working within each of us
and that we all share.

We are all on the same
spiritual journey together.
A journey that is written by each of us,
as our own job description.

DAILY DEFLECTION – QUESTIONS

1. Write out your job description. Remember, it's unique to you.

2. How might your job description change in the months and years ahead?

Are coffee shops the new churches?

Coffee Time

It used to be in churches
with stained glass windows and stillness
where our grandparents found respite.

For quiet, peace, reflection and rest,
it is now to the coffee shop,
with its soft chairs and quiet corners,
that we go.

The carefully designed colour schemes of
Caffè Nero or Starbucks soothe our minds.
The lighting creates a mood to help us relax.

But God is just as at home in a coffee shop.
For to rest and reflect
is really what matters for body and soul.

God is with us wherever we are,
not just in churches or Costas.

DAILY DEFLECTION – QUESTIONS

1. When will you take some time to rest and reflect today?

2. Is it coffee time yet?

What is your lifetime cashflow position?

Cash Flow

The birds of the air
get their food.
The money will come.

The fish in the water
get their food.
The money will come.

All of my life
I've had food.
The money has come.

DAILY DEFLECTION – QUESTIONS

1. What does your life cash flow look like?

2. Where and how has the money come?

3. What does this say to you about your future hopes and dreams?

How should I write my affirmations?

Affirmations

Every day I say my affirmations.
I call them my daily reminders as they help me
to focus on all that is important to me
and all I want to see happen in my life.

My daily reminders cover every aspect of my life
and everything I could ever hope for:
work, opportunities, health, income, family,
personality, relationships and spirituality.

They are written in the present or past tense.
I am, I have, I own, I earn, I live...
I say my daily reminders
every morning and every night.

I can see every outcome in detail,
and watch as the results unfold.
For I am fulfilling my personal purpose
in all that I do today.

DAILY DEFLECTION – QUESTIONS

1. Write out your daily statements in the present or past tense – *I am, I have, I own, I earn, I live...*

2. Include everything that matters to you.

Can we apply lateral thinking to our lives?

Lateral Thinking

The sunflower seed
does not worry about
being planted in the ground
to wither and die.

For it has been told
that it will become
something unimaginable
for such a little seed.

We too have been told that
we will become something
incredible and unimaginable.
We are all sunflowers.

DAILY DEFLECTION – QUESTIONS

1. Without light, the sunflower seed cannot grow. Who, what or where is your light?

2. Each of us is already something incredible and unimaginable. How can we help our fellow sunflowers to grow?

What's your special offer?

Special Offer

Buy one – get one free.
Green Shield Stamps.
Nectar Card.
Air Miles.

Buy three – cheapest one free.
Smart Rewards.
Premier Points.
Avios.

Clubcard.
Loyalty rewards.
Tiger Tokens.
50% off.

Weekend Special.
Happy Hour.
Double points.
Gift Certificates.

Cashback.
Frequent Flyer.
Christmas Club.
Blue Cross Day.

Why do more
of the same?
Make an offer
that really matters.

DAILY DEFLECTION – QUESTIONS

1. What is your offer?

2. Why does it really matter?

Is there a power point?

Power Point

I will find a
moment of silence,
somewhere in this
busy day.

At some point
I will be able to stop,
rest, and give myself
some space.

Just to be who I am,
away from all the noise,
and demands
of the world.

At some point,
I will find
a moment of silence,
in this busy day.

DAILY DEFLECTION – QUESTIONS

1. When is your power point today?

2. What will this moment of silence offer you?

3. What will be in the presentation?

Do you operate on autopilot?

Autopilot

My thoughts are
all over the place.
I flit from one thing
to another.

I've learnt to go with this,
and not become too engaged
in any one thought,
but to flit onwards.

For me, reflection or contemplation
are not about breathing techniques
or trying to empty my brain
of all thoughts.

Rather, they are about meandering,
and using the thoughts
that come along
simply as stepping stones.

For if I am patient
and sit here,
I will get to
where I should be.

DAILY DEFLECTION – QUESTIONS

1. Take some time today and place your trust in your autopilot.
   Give it time to take you to where you should be.

What are core values?

Core Values

Stay at the core
and not at the periphery.
For all potential
lies at the core.

We can get ambushed
by worldliness,
by necessity,
by rights,
by fairness,
by ambition,
by vanity,
by self-importance.

Stay at the core.

DAILY DEFLECTION – QUESTIONS

1. What are your core values?

2. How can these values help you maintain your centre?

Retreat 9 – Notes and Key Points

Day 1

_____
_____
_____

Day 2

_____
_____
_____

Day 3

_____
_____
_____

Day 4

_____
_____
_____

Day 5

_____

_____

_____

Day 6

_____

_____

_____

Day 7

_____

_____

_____

Overall thoughts about the week

_____

_____

_____

_____

Points to take with me on the journey

_____

_____

_____

_____

Personal Development Retreat

20

How can we reduce stress in our lives?

Stress Management

When I get overwhelmed,
thinking about all that
I have to do,
I now stop and smile.

You see, I've learned
that although it seems
so important now,
it will be different next week.

I step back and smile.
I decide to do what I can,
go with the flow,
and just be happy in myself.

DAILY DEFLECTION – QUESTIONS

1. When do you tend to feel overwhelmed?

2. What will it all look like next week?

Where do you want to make a difference?

On Purpose

Of course, we are busy
with lots to do.
Our families and work make
demands all the time.

It is easy to be
in reactive mode.
Sometimes it is hard enough
just to get through the day.

Often, we don't get everything
done that we should.
It can be difficult to
even think about our purpose.

We sense, deep down,
why we are here.
And we know what is
really important to us.

We still want to
make a difference.
This may be about poverty,
or children or the environment.

It may be about illness
or helping others.
But our big dreams can
get swamped by daily demands.

This, however, is
far from the truth.
For every single thing we do
comes from our purpose.

Every good thought
can produce a response from us
that is visible, and then
magnified through others.

Everything we do is on purpose.
So, let's be clear
about what is
really important to us.

For in our kindness
and compassion, we achieve all.
In our busy day, everything
we do is on purpose.

So, look beyond the activities
and trust in yourself.
For everything you do
is as it should be.

At different points in our lives
we have our calls.
And each time they're met with
the same core response.

The right actions come
from each of us as they should.
And everything we do
is on purpose.

DAILY DEFLECTION – QUESTIONS

1. Where would you like to make a difference?

2. What exactly would you like to see happen?

What is the best Daily Deflection routine?

Daily Deflection

Treat each day
like a race
and run,
run to win.

See the finish line
and go for it.
Go fast.
Run to win.

Start fast.
Get faster.
Keep going.
Run to win.

Who knows what
you might do
if you run.
Run to win.

Go past the finish line.
All is possible.
Run today.
Run to win.

DAILY DEFLECTION – QUESTIONS

1. What is your race today?

2. Where is your finish line?

3. Are you running now?

How can we create a masterpiece?

Masterpiece

Don't just create new pieces.
Don't just look for more pieces.
Don't just revamp the pieces
you already have.
Don't just reorganise
and move all your pieces around.

Throw them all away –
all your pieces.
Clear the table.
Start with a different picture.
Start today from scratch.
A blank canvas.

DAILY DEFLECTION – QUESTIONS

1. Describe the masterpiece that you will create from today.

2. What are the pieces you need to make this real?

Why is dying like a rollercoaster ride?

Rollercoaster

Dying is like
a rollercoaster ride
with the kids.

You know you've got to do it.
It's going to be scary,
but all will be okay
when it's over.

DAILY DEFLECTION – QUESTIONS

1. Why are children and young people often so much more adventurous and brave than older people in a theme park?

2. What actually happens on the rollercoaster of dying?

What is turnover?

Turnover

It was so much darker
when I awoke this morning.
Summer is slipping away.
It's cold and raining.

I marvel at the continuous
and seamless transition
of the seasons,
year after year.

They tell me that we also move
through different phases,
and that we too are continuously
renewed and reborn.

DAILY DEFLECTION – QUESTIONS

1. What phase of your life are you moving into?

2. When you look back over the last year, how have you changed
   or developed?

What are personal standard operating procedures?

Standard Operating Procedure

For twenty years I cut the grass the same way
from the back door to the beach and back again,
stripes leading outwards from the back door,
taking me to the beach and back again.

Today, I cut the grass a different way.
I don't know why – it just happened.
I cut the grass from left to right
and then right to left.

Starting at the back door
and slowly getting closer to the beach,
without going back to the house.
I had stripes across the lawn,
rather than up and down.

Today, after twenty years,
I cut the grass in a different way.

DAILY DEFLECTION – QUESTIONS

1. What is your routine or standard operating procedure?

2. What might you change – just to get a different perspective?

How long is a settling-in period?

Probation Period

We've only been here
for a few days,
but it feels like months.
I feel like we are now well settled
in this place.

We've been in this house
for a few years,
but it seems like a lifetime.
I feel like we are now well settled
in the area.

Although I've been around
for fifty years or so,
it all seems like yesterday.
I feel like I'm only just settling
into my life.

I'm just starting to feel comfortable
with what is going on,
and who I am.
I feel like I'm beginning to settle
into my life.

387

DAILY DEFLECTION – QUESTIONS

1. How well are you settling into your life?

2. What areas are you comfortable with?

3. What areas are you not totally at ease with yet?

Have you synced the different parts of your life?

Timekeeper

The village clock says 11:52
and chimes three times.

An hour later,
the village clock says 11:52
and chimes four times.

DAILY DEFLECTION – QUESTIONS

1. How well are you keeping time?

2. How might you stop your clock?

What are your words of encouragement?

Vocational Guidance

Be gracious.
Be kind.
Listen.
Ask questions.
Smile.

Be positive,
no matter what.
Find the good in every situation.
Search for alternatives,
even if you cannot see any.

Do not boast.
Do not take the credit.
Be humble;
after all, your success
is because of others.

Recognise that you are not perfect
and that this, in itself, is perfect.
Accept that others are not perfect,
and that is the way
it is meant to be.

You do not have to know everything.
Just work with those you can help,
and with others who can help you.
Love plays to people's strengths.
Discover and celebrate the talents of others.

Your workplace is the whole world.
Your task is to reach out to all,
for you are responsible for everyone.
This is not an impossible task.
It is your gift of compassion to those in need.

Be ambitious
for all that you can be.
Remember that you can
achieve absolutely anything
with the right support.

Surprise others –
make them laugh.
Do the unexpected.
Make every day different
and every meeting memorable.
Make every customer
feel amazing with your smile.

Respond to unhelpful people with kindness.
Answer aggression with politeness.
Stick to your own framework of love,
no matter what difficulties arise.
For all things will pass.

Stay young,
no matter how old you are.
Be wise and listen,
no matter how young you are –
always.

What you do today is your legacy.
Use every moment.
Explore.
Wonder at the sunrise, the water
and the smile of the child.

Embrace those you love
every day.
Hug them and tell them
that they are truly amazing.
Tell them you love them.

Your children
will teach you everything
you need to know.
Your grandchildren
will teach you even more.

Remember that you are working
in every minute.
And being rewarded
with the gift of life.
Never work just for money,
for time is so precious.

Every person is a star,
every conversation an inspiration.
Capture value from everything,
for it has all been given to you as a gift.
Be thankful.

Your work is you.
It isn't an office building or a factory.
Take your work into every situation,
as a force for good,
as a champion of love.

You are a fountain of love.
You can choose
to be majestic
or to keep your tap turned off.
You are the fountain of all love.

All love can flow through you.
All the love that has ever been
and ever will be
is connected to you
and through you.

Your health will not always be good
so never take it for granted.
Waking up in the morning
is the most amazing gift ever,
for one day it will cease.

Be bold.
Be brave.
Be daring.
Be adventurous. Be creative –
for love.

Shake the tree and rattle the cage.
How else will you know
if apples will fall or the lion will roar?
Then gather the apples
and open the cage.

Don't accept half measures.
Don't settle for anything less than brilliant.
Bring out the best in everyone.
For if it is worth doing,
it's worth doing right.

Don't be self-sufficient!
Build amazing relationships everyday:
with your partner, your family,
your community
and your many workplaces.

Decide where you're going.
Imagine all that you should be.
Focus on this each day.
Don't get distracted.
Stay your course and claim that prize.

Just because it hasn't been done before
doesn't mean you can't do it.
Just because everyone else has failed
doesn't mean you will.
Just because others say something
doesn't mean it's true.
Listen to yourself.

Go for a walk
on your own
every day.
Sit in silence
and try not to think.

Forgive yourself –
always.
Stop beating yourself up.
You are perfect as you are.
You have nothing to prove to anyone.

Be thankful every single night.
Recognise all that has happened
and the fact that you were part of all
that has happened today.
You played your part in
the theatre of the world.

Sometimes it's good to
act fast.
Other times it's good to sit
and do nothing.
Go with the flow.

You are not on your own.
You are not alone,
even in your darkest moments.
All times will pass
and love will continue to grow.

Be successful before 10 o'clock each day.
Always say yes.
Ask for help, for it's a sign of strength.
Build linkages
and enable others to play their part.
Be enthusiastic in your work
and smile.

You are amazing!
Use your voice
and say what is important to you.
Decide on your purpose
and play every day
with possibilities.

DAILY DEFLECTION – QUESTIONS

1. What advice would you pass on to others?

2. What words of encouragement have you for others?

Retreat 20 – Notes and Key Points

Day 1

_____

_____

_____

Day 2

_____

_____

_____

Day 3

_____

_____

_____

Day 4

_____

_____

_____

Day 5

_____

_____

_____

Day 6

_____

_____

_____

Day 7

_____

_____

_____

Overall thoughts about the week

_____

_____

_____

_____

Points to take with me on the journey

_____

_____

_____

_____

Evaluation and Review

Many congratulations for working through the Personal Development Retreats in this book!

Let us pause for a few minutes and review your learning and outcomes. You don't need to answer all of the questions below, but they can help you to harvest different aspects of your learning and capture steps on your personal development journey.

1. Retreats

- Which were your favourite Retreats?

- Which Retreat was most useful or had most impact for you?

- What was the most rewarding thing about doing the Retreats?

- How have the Retreats helped you?

2. Daily Deflections

- Can you list your Top 10 Daily Deflections?

- What was your favourite Daily Deflection overall?

- Are there any Daily Deflections you would like to revisit or continue to spend time with?

3. Recurring Themes

- When you wrote notes, what did you write about?

- What are the key themes that emerged for you?

4. Personal Learning

- What have been the main learning points for you over the last weeks?

- What have you uncovered about yourself from this process?

5. Personal Impact

- How has your thinking shifted? In what ways/areas?

- How do you feel *in yourself* or *about yourself*, having worked on the Retreats?

- How have you grown or changed over the last few weeks?

- What is different about you?

6. Personal Action Plan

- What will be your key action points moving forward?

- When you look back in 12 months' time, what will be the one key thing that you will have achieved or that will have changed?

- How are you going to continue and build upon your Personal Development Retreat process? (Check out the other books in this series.)

7. Your 100-Word Summary

Finally, you may wish to bring all this together as one snapshot. Use the Notes Pages at the end of each Retreat and the questions above to write a 100-Word Summary on this stage of your Personal Development Retreat Journey. Refer to this as you move forward. Use this to encourage and motivate yourself and to be grateful for all that you are.

Evaluation and Review – Notes

Where do we go from here?

I hope that you will continue the daily routine that you have established and continue your own personal development journey. Here are some ideas for you:

Continue with your process of reflection
Now that you are developing the habit of taking some time with yourself each day, you can continue and extend this practice. You might revisit some Exercises in this book or perhaps relook at the ones you may have passed over the first time around. Numerous people have said that they have gained new insights when they have completed the same retreat a second time.

Retreat mode
The personal development retreat format offers us the flexibility to weave our process of reflection into all that we do. When we're walking in the park, we may find it natural to switch into retreat mode. When sitting waiting for the train, we may find that we have a few moments to reflect on the bigger journey. Just before we drift off to sleep, we may have a quiet recollection on the day's events. All these moments can help us to develop an ongoing conversation with our inner self, understand more about who we are and experience each day with greater joy and gratitude.

Retreat moments

Many people also build their fabric of Retreat moments by using quotes from famous people, reflecting on some words from a sacred text, dipping into a book of poetry or reading inspirational stories of people who have gone before us.

Continue with your Journal

Try and take a few moments each day to sit and write something in your Journal. Continue to write! This may be when you're having a coffee, a quick break at your desk or at a set time every day.

Personal Development Retreat books

There are more books in this series, so you've plenty of Retreats to work through!

- *Daily Deflections – Take ten minutes to transform your life with Personal Development Retreats, wherever you are Volume 2: Retreats 21–40*

- *Daily Deflections – Take ten minutes to transform your life with Personal Development Retreats, wherever you are Volume 3: Retreats 41–60*

Do check out my personal website for other personal development books and resources: www.desmccabe.com

Author Note

Thank you for exploring these Daily Deflections. If you have found these Personal Development Retreats helpful, then please drop me a note (contact details below).
It would be great to hear from you!

If you can, please leave a short review on Amazon, as this will encourage others to spend a little time on their personal development.

I wish you continued joy and happiness in all that you are and all that you do. Keep going with your personal development journey – every day!

Take care,
Des

Contact Des McCabe

You can get in touch with me here:

Author Website: www.desmccabe.com
Training Website: www.workitout.info
Email: diversiton@gmail.com
Phone: 44 7717 203325
Amazon Author Page: https://amzn.to/35Z4jr0
(all the latest books)
LinkedIn: www.linkedin.com/in/desmccabe
(let's connect!)

Acknowledgement

I'd like to say a very special 'thank you' to three amazing people, Diane Page (my wonderful editor who guides me in so many ways), Gail Cassidy (my fellow author who encouraged me to keep writing these) and Pauline McCabe (who accepted my new habit of getting up at 6 o'clock every morning!). This series of 'daily deflections' would not have happened without them. Thank you.

About Des

Des McCabe is one of the leading experts on inclusion and personal development.

In the early part of his career, Des founded TBG, which grew to become the largest independent training organisation in the UK. When the company was sold in 1995, it was finding jobs for 5,000 long-term unemployed and helping 4,000 people to get qualifications every year.

Des's expertise in the field of job creation led to him becoming an advisor to the British, Irish, US, Argentinian, Romanian and Albanian governments on employment and inclusion. He received formal recognition as one of the leading job-creation entrepreneurs from *Europe's 500*, Europe's most prominent body of entrepreneurs.

Des served as Chair of the European Union's cross-border Interreg training group in Northern Ireland, and as Chair of the EU Border Training Bureau. He was an advisor to the Irish and US Governments in the early stages of the Northern Ireland Peace Process and went on to design the *Peace Builder* training programme with US Special Envoy Senator George Mitchell's Northern Ireland Fund for Reconciliation.

Beyond his professional achievements, Des established and raised funding for The Training Trust, an international charity set up to meet the humanitarian needs of children in Romanian orphanages. He has assisted with Comic Relief projects in Kenya and supported a range of anti-poverty initiatives in Ghana and Madagascar.

In 2003 Des founded Diversiton as a social enterprise. Its Inclusion Calendar is used internationally by hundreds of organisations. The annual International Inclusion Awards and the Diversity Champion Awards are also administered by Diversiton.

In 2011 Hay House published Des's ground-breaking book, *Work it Out!: How to Find the Work You Always Wanted in a Shifting Jobs Market*, which led to the development of the Inverted Pyramid methodology.

From 2014 the Irish Government, as well as numerous agencies and businesses worldwide, supported a wide range of *Work it Out!* initiatives to build inclusion and promote sustainability within local communities and workplaces.

From 2019, Des became well-known for his experience in licensing, helping many colleagues to offer their training courses and services across the world.

410

In 2020, Des began writing Personal Development Retreats, leading to the first series of Daily Deflections being published in 2023.

Printed in Great Britain
by Amazon